talking

the

TALK

Spanish

MICK WEBB

Series Editor: Alwena Lamping

Published by BBC Active, an imprint of Educational Publishers LLP, part of the Pearson Education Group, Edinburgh Gate, Harlow, Essex CM20 2JE, England.

© Educational Publishers LLP 2017

BBC logo © BBC 1996. BBC and BBC ACTIVE are trademarks of the British Broadcasting Corporation.

First published 2017.
5 4 3 2 1

ISBN 978-1-4066-8468-1

Publisher: Debbie Marshall
Development editors: Esther Sahagún, Elena Salas
Layout: Reality Premedia Services
Cover design: Two Associates
Cover photograph: © iStock.com/rognar
Illustrations: © Mark Duffin
Project editor: Emma Brown
Proofreading: Ruth Manteca Tahoces
Contributor: Siân Stratton-Brown
Audio producer: Colette Thomson, Footstep Productions Ltd.

Printed and bound by Neografia, Slovakia.

The Publisher's policy is to use paper manufactured from sustainable forests.

contents

introduction

Talking the TALK Spanish is BBC Active's latest addition to the bestselling **TALK** series. It is about social conversation: not just small talk but getting to know people and their lives, sharing information, opinions and anecdotes, making plans, talking about aspirations and obligations – and more.

An audio component complements the book and is available for you to download from www.bbcactivelanguages.com/TTS.

Who is it for?

It's for people of all ages who are learning Spanish or who are familiar with the basics, and whose ambition is to be able to chat to people in Spanish, whether someone they've met on holiday, a business contact, extended family, a fellow enthusiast, a neighbour or anyone else.

The contents are also ideal for someone who has followed a course but would like to update their Spanish and extend the range of what they can say.

How does it work?

It is based on the principles of successful conversation. Everyday conversation hangs on a relatively small number of **core linguistic structures** which provide the framework for what we want to say. The potential of this framework is realised by building on it, so **personalised vocabulary building** is a priority. This book contains hundreds of examples, using **varied and contemporary language**.

Conversation works better if you have the **strategies to keep it flowing**. And it's easier when you're confident that what you're saying sounds **natural and up to date**, and when you know that you'll be **readily understood**.

Is it easy to use?

The approach is hands-on, to enable you to adapt what you're learning so that it's **personal and relevant** to you. Content is presented in **manageable steps**, with page headings showing clearly what the focus is. Core linguistic structures are generously illustrated and explained with the hallmark

TALK clarity. Focused word banks, placed just where you need them, allow you to practise, adapt and **personalise the language structures**: there are frequent suggestions on how you might do this.

The design allows learning Spanish to fit into a busy lifestyle: this is a book that can be dipped into a page or two at a time. The pages are grouped into 10 chapters, each of which ends with conversations that bring the language you're learning to life and a checkpoint which serves as revision and as an aid to remembering the contents.

How does the audio fit in?

The Spanish presenters of the audio have clear aims:

- **helping you to pronounce Spanish correctly**, since conversation is more enjoyable when both sides understand each other without endless repetition. They guide you through the sounds of Spanish, focusing on the ones that English speakers often struggle with. They do this with material selected from each chapter, **reinforcing the core language structures**. They're supported in the book by how to sound Spanish, a guide to the sounds and stress patterns of Spanish.

- **developing your listening skills**, since conversation is as much to do with listening as talking. Each chapter ends with some informal conversations; these are printed in your book on the Talking the TALK page, and the Audio Support Pack offers suggestions on how to make the most of them.

How do I access the audio?

To download the audio, go to www.bbcactivelanguages.com/TTS.

For maximum flexibility, you can download the complete script including the conversations and you can download the conversations separately, entirely in Spanish, for intensive listening.

The **Audio Support Pack** is also available from www.bbcactivelanguages.com/TTS. It includes full transcripts plus guidance and activities on how to make the most of the conversations.

> BBC Active would like to thank all the language tutors who contributed to the planning of Talking the TALK. The concept is based on your suggestions and feedback.

the basics

grammar terms

To get to the point when you can hold your own in a conversation, you don't need to know complex and detailed grammatical terminology. But familiarity with the basic terms can fast-track you to that point because it allows you to make sense of explanations of how Spanish works.

The ten definitions on this page will take you a very long way. You don't have to learn them all now: just remember they're here for quick reference. If you decide you would like to know more, there's a fuller list on pages 154–156.

Nouns are the words for living beings, things, places and abstract concepts: *boy, Rachel, engineer, mosquito, computer, house, Madrid, time, strategy*.

Articles are *the, a/an* and *some*.

A **pronoun** is used instead of a noun, and saves having to repeat that noun: *Where's Theo? He's with a friend; I saw them earlier*.

Adjectives are words used to describe a noun or a pronoun: *good wine; strong red wine; my wine; that wine; it is Spanish; it was superb*.

Verbs are words like *to eat, to live, to sleep, go, listen, have, want, be, die*, that relate to doing and being. In English you can put *to* in front of a verb: *to eat*.

In a dictionary, Spanish verbs are listed in the **infinitive**, the equivalent of *to eat*. Nearly all Spanish infinitives end in **-ar**, **-er** or **-ir**: **presentar** *to present*, **responder** *to reply*, **decidir** *to decide*.

The **-ar**, **-er** and **-ir** at the end of infinitives are called – understandably – **verb endings**. They're significant in Spanish: they change to carry a variety of information.

The **tense** of a verb refers to when it's happening, e.g. present tense, future tense. The perfect and imperfect tenses refer to the past.

Most verbs, nouns and adjectives follow patterns: these are defined as **regular**. Ones that deviate from the patterns are called **irregular** and have to be learnt separately. English too has irregularities, e.g. *boy/boys* but *child/children*; *work/work**ed*** but *speak/spoke*.

the main differences between Spanish and English

There are many similarities between Spanish and English, and some essential differences too. It helps to be prepared for those.

- One conspicuous contrast is the way adjectives often come after nouns in Spanish: **parque nacional** *national park*, **inteligencia artificial** *artificial intelligence*. Also, words like *it, us, her, them* usually come before a verb not after it: **Yo lo creo** *I believe it*.

- Every single Spanish noun – not just the words for people and animals – is either masculine (m) or feminine (f). There's no sense of *it*, not even for things like cars, food, sport or days of the week. Many, but by no means all, masculine nouns end in -o and feminine nouns in -a.

- Words linked to a noun have to be masculine or feminine to agree with it. *The*: **el menú** (m), **la música** (f), **los vinos** (m pl), **las ideas** (f pl). An adjective in a dictionary has the masculine singular ending, but it changes to agree with the noun: **el menú español, la música española, los vinos españoles, las ideas españolas**.

- **Uno** and **una** which mean *one* or *a/an* have a plural: **unos** and **unas**. These mean *some/a few* but they're not always translated into English.

- Spanish has five words for *you*, **tú, usted, vosotros, vosotras** and **ustedes**, depending on who you're talking to. So every sentence or question containing *you* can be phrased in five slightly different ways.

- In the English *Do you speak other languages? Yes, I speak Russian*, the verb *speak* in the question is repeated in the answer. In the Spanish equivalent **¿Hablas otros idiomas? Sí, hablo ruso**, the verb has a different ending in the answer. A verb in Spanish changes its ending more widely than in English depending on who is carrying it out.

- Because it's clear from its ending who's implementing the verb, the words *I, we, you, he/she, it, they* aren't essential and are omitted more often than not. This can sound quite strange until you get used to it.

- Perhaps the most surprising difference is that Spanish has two ways of saying *I am*. As a very general rule of thumb, **soy** is for fixed aspects such as nationality while **estoy** is for aspects that can change such as mood and state of health; it's also the one to use for position/location. **Soy** and **estoy** come from the verbs **ser** and **estar**, and the same principles apply to all their other parts, e.g. *she is, we are, you are*.

how to
sound Spanish

The sounds and rhythm of Spanish are not the same as English but, with the right knowledge and focused practice, it's entirely feasible for an English speaker to speak Spanish with an accent easily understood by native speakers, regardless of where in Spain or Latin America they come from.

The starting point is listening, to as many different voices and accents as possible. There are different levels of listening: more often than not you're listening in order to understand **what's** being said, but you can also train yourself to listen in order to hear **how** something is being said. It doesn't even matter that you don't understand everything, what you're doing is getting a feel for the rhythm and overall sound of Spanish. When you hear many Spaniards speaking English, you'll recognise that same rhythm – and this is what you're aiming to recreate.

Spanish sounds are not difficult for English speakers if you

● learn how to pronounce the letters of the alphabet and key combinations of letters. This takes relatively little time because the sounds are consistent and don't vary from one word to the next, unlike English;

● practise and keep practising until what you say is what you hear. It's not enough to say things in your head; you need to say them out loud so that your speech organs – e.g. vocal cords, tongue, lips, teeth, soft and hard palate – are working and adapting to Spanish sounds.

The Talking the TALK audio download, available from www.bbcactivelanguages.com/TTS, is there to support you. But before sampling the audio, have a look at the next few pages, which summarise the fundamentals of pronunciation, stress and rhythm.

vowels

In English, vowels sound different according to which word they're in, e.g.

a: cart, care, paw, woman
o: one, bone, done, gone

This doesn't happen in Spanish; the five Spanish vowels are always pronounced in the same way. Each is sounded cleanly and crisply, with nothing added.

a   as in the English cat, father
e   as in pen
i   as in bee, machine
o   like the English *not* without the *t*; this is how to pronounce **no** in Spanish
u   as in blue, crude

vowels next to each other

a, **e** and **o** are strong vowels, while **i** and **u** are weak.

Two strong vowels together both have equal weight, or stress:
creer *creh·ehr*, **idea** *ee·deh·ah*

When two weak vowels are together, the stress is on the second.
ruido *roo·ee·doh,* **seguir** *seg·eer*

A strong and weak vowel together merge into a single sound with the stress on the strong vowel:
puedo *pooeh·doh,* **aura** *ahoo·rah*

Exceptions are marked with an accent: **día** *dee·ah*

The majority of Spanish words end in a vowel. These are never swallowed or mute, which means that words that look identical to English words are pronounced differently.

> **grave** *serious* is pronounced *grah·veh*
> **pausa** *pause, interval* is pronounced *pow·sah*
> **sublime** *sublime* is pronounced *soo·blee·meh*

consonants

Some consonants sound similar in Spanish and English, but the following are different.

c + most letters sounds like the English *k*: **c**afé, **c**lima.

ch	is like the English *ch* in *chimney*: **c**hico *boy*, **c**hica *girl*, **ch**orizo.
c + e or i	in much of Spain is pronounced like *th* in *thanks*: **gracias** *thanks*, **plac**er *pleasure*. But in Latin America and the South of Spain, **ce** and **ci** sound like *ce* in *cereal*.
cc	is pronounced *kth*: **direcc**ión *address, direction*.
b and v	sound virtually the same. At the beginning of a word they're like the *b* in *beat*: **v**amos *let's go*, **v**enga *come on*. Between two vowels, the sound is softer, made by just touching the lips together: **deb**er *to owe*, **lav**ar *to wash*.
d	is a soft sound when it's between vowels or at the end of a word, like *th* in *then*: **casad**o *married*, **ciudad** *city*. But at the beginning of a word, it's like *d* in *day* **d**ía.
g + e or i	comes from the back of the throat, sounding rather like the *hh* sound in *loch*: **g**enial *great*, **g**inebra *gin*.
h	is not pronounced: it has no sound of its own in Spanish: **h**ospital.
j	is pronounced in the same way as g + e/i.
ll	is usually like the *y* sound in *yes*: **ca**ll**e**, *street*. But in some regions it's like *lli* in the middle of *billion*, and in Argentina it's more of a *jh* sound.
ñ	known as a **tilde**, **ñ** is pronounced like *ny* in *canyon*: **maña**na.
r/ rr	The only really challenging Spanish sound for English speakers is the pronunciation of **rr** or a single **r** at the beginning of a word. It's made by vibrating the tip of your tongue against the top front of your mouth, practically on the back of the teeth, which produces a trilling sound. A single **r** in other parts of a word is not vibrated like the double one.
s	always has a soft sound like the English *ss* in *fuss*.
z	in much of Spain sounds like the English *th* in *thanks*: **la plaz**a *the square*. But in Latin America and the South of Spain, it is like the *ce* in *cereal*.

stress

There are straightforward rules governing where the stress falls in Spanish words. Very often, it falls in a different place from the equivalent word in English.

A word ending in a vowel has the stress on the second to last syllable: **adulto** *adult*, **presidente** *president*.

A word ending in a consonant other than **n** or **s** has the stress on the last syllable: **capaz** *capable*, **ciudad** *city*, **color** *colour*, **controlar** *to control*, **nacional** *national* ... but **examen** *exam*, **coliflores** *cauliflowers*.

There are exceptions to these two rules. In writing, they're indicated by an accent over the stressed vowel: **árbol** *tree*, **teléfono** *phone*, **marítimo** *maritime*, **conversación** *conversation*, **azúcar** *sugar*.

In written Spanish, an accent is also used to distinguish single syllable words which have two different meanings: **sí** *yes*, **si** *if*; **más** *more*, **mas** *but*; **el** *the*, **él** *he*; **sé** *I know*, **se** *himself/herself* etc. It also marks out question words: **cuando** *when*, **¿cuándo?** *when?*

intonation/rhythm

Pronunciation is about more than individual words. It involves the rhythm and intonation of whole sentences: how the voice rises at the end of a question and falls in an exclamation; how it varies when registering different emotions.

Getting this right is largely a matter of listening and imitating. When actors are learning an accent, after mastering the key sounds they focus on the rhythm of a language. They also watch how mouths and faces move, and what gestures people make with their hands and shoulders when they speak. When they themselves start speaking, they exaggerate the sounds and gestures, with a view to toning them down later.

uno
first impressions

Despite the openness and approachability of most native Spanish speakers, there are codes of behaviour underlying the way people communicate, which depend on social context, age and hierarchy.

In Spanish, you're immediately faced with a decision about which version of *you* to use – **tú** or **usted** – so that you don't unknowingly get off on the wrong foot with people you meet.

There are also common courtesies, ways of addressing and greeting people, which help to oil the wheels of daily conversation. It's useful to know, for instance, that when you go into someone else's house or welcome a Spanish person into yours, the expression used is **Estás en tu casa** *Make yourself at home*, literally *You're in your own home*.

Many traditional and hierarchical terms of address have been discarded by the democratic Spain that emerged following Franco's death in 1975. However, in much of Latin America, in Mexico for example, there's still a preference for formality and what often appears to foreigners to be old-fashioned courtesy.

choosing between tú and usted

Unlike English, which has only one word for *you*, Spanish has five.

tú	used with someone you know well and call by their first name, as well as people you've just met who are about your age or younger. Children are always **tú**. It's about being casual, familiar and informal.
usted	for use with strangers or with somebody you've already met but don't know particularly well, a person who's clearly older than you are, who's in a senior position in work or towards whom you want to appear respectful. This is the word for more formal situations. It is usually shortened in writing to **Ud.** or **Vd.** and derives from an old Spanish term of respect: **Vuestra Merced** *Your Grace*.
vosotros	used instead of **tú** when talking to more than one person. **Vosotros** becomes vosotras if these people are female.
ustedes	written **Uds.** or **Vds.**, this is the plural of **usted** and is the formal way to talk to two or more people.

In parts of Latin America, notably Argentina, you'll hear the word **vos** used instead of **tú**.

The verb changes according to which *you* is being used.

	How are you?	When are you arriving?
tú	¿Cómo estás?	¿Cuándo llegas?
usted	¿Cómo está?	¿Cuándo llega?
vosotros/as	¿Cómo estáis?	¿Cuándo llegáis?
ustedes	¿Cómo están?	¿Cuándo llegan?

Widespread use of **tú** is becoming more acceptable, particularly in Spain, and is the norm on social media and among groups of young people. But if you use **tú** straightaway with an older person or an official, they might well perceive it as over-familiarity. If you're not sure whether to use **tú** or **usted**, opt for **usted**. You can sometimes take your cue from the other person, although you don't necessarily use **tú** with someone who's calling you **tú** — it all depends on who that person is. If **tú** is more appropriate than **usted**, a native speaker will soon suggest ¿**Nos tuteamos?** *Shall we use tú?* or **Trátame/Háblame de tú** *Call me tú*.

addressing someone properly

Señor and **señora** followed by a name equate to *Mr* and *Mrs,* but they're also used widely without a name. It's considered a basic courtesy to add them to greetings — something which has no equivalent in English:
Buenos días, señor/señora *Good morning.*

They have a plural:
Buenos días, señores. *Good morning.*
Adiós, señoras. *Goodbye.*

Although **señorita** is still occasionally used to address unmarried women, its use is in decline and it's best to say **señora**. **Señorito**, the male equivalent, tends to have the very specific meaning of *spoilt rich kid/young man.*

Don and **doña** are respectful and rather antiquated terms that you'll still hear used with the first names of older people. **Doña Perfecta** is the title of a famous nineteenth-century novel by Benito Pérez Galdós, the Spanish equivalent of Charles Dickens. **Nadie** means *nobody*, and in colloquial speech **Es un don nadie** is used to describe someone with delusions of grandeur.

Spanish names

Spanish people have two **apellidos** *surnames*, as they inherit the first **apellido** of each of their parents, e.g. **Arantxa Sánchez Vicario**. When talking, though, people generally just use the first surname: **Hola, soy Arantxa Sánchez** *Hello, I'm Arantxa Sánchez.*

Amongst women of older generations, you'll find quite surprising first names with religious connotations, such as **Soledad** *Solitude*, **Concepción** *Conception*, **Socorro** *Help* and **Inmaculada** *Immaculate*.

First names are routinely abbreviated. **Inmaculada** becomes **Inma**, while someone called **Concepción** is usually addressed as **Conchi** or **Concha**. The shortened names aren't always easy to guess. The female name **Dolores** becomes **Loli** or **Lola** and the male name **Francisco** nearly always turns into **Paco**, while someone called **José** is often known as **Pepe**!

greeting people confidently

hello

Buenos días. *Hello. Good morning.*
Buenas tardes. *Hello. Good afternoon. Good evening.*
Buenas noches. *Goodnight.*
Hola. *Hello. Hi.*

Buenos días is used until midday, when **buenas tardes** takes over.
Buenas tardes is used until around dinner time, which in Spain tends to be eaten late: about 9 p.m. After that, you use **buenas noches**.
Hola can be used at any time, either on its own or in phrases like **Hola chicos** *Hi guys,* **¡Hola guapa!** *Hi gorgeous!*

Buenas or **Muy buenas** is an informal greeting like *Morning* or *Afternoon*.

Greetings tend to be followed by a title or a name.
Buenos días, señor/señora.
Buenos días, Conchi.
Buenas tardes, señora Martínez.
Hola, Paco.

how are you?

¿Cómo estás/está/estáis/están? *How are you?* (**tú/usted/vosotros/ustedes**)
¿Qué tal? *How are you?*
¿Qué tal, chicos/chicas? *How are you, guys/girls?*
¿Cómo va? *How's it going?*

Bien, gracias. *Fine, thank you.*
... ¿y tú/usted/vosotros/vosotras/ustedes? *... and you?*

While **Bien, gracias** is a perfectly adequate reply to **¿Cómo estás?**, there are plenty of other options, such as:
Muy bien. *Really well.*
¡Genial! *Great!*
Bastante bien, gracias. *Not so bad, thanks.*
Regular. *OK.*
Vamos tirando. *Getting by ... can't complain.*
¡Ahí estamos/andamos! *We're still here!*
¡Fatal! *Terrible!*

farewells

goodbye

Adiós. *Goodbye.*
You'll also hear **adiós** used as a greeting when two acquaintances pass in the street but don't have time to stop and chat.

Buenas noches. *Goodnight.*
¡Que descanses! *Sleep well!* lit. *Rest well!*
¡Que te/le vaya bien! *Take care! See you!* (**tú/usted**)
¡Que te/le vaya bonito! *Have a good day! See you!* (**tú/usted**) (used more in Latin America)

Buenos días, **buenas tardes** and **buenas noches** can also be used to say *goodbye,* with the sense of *Have a good day/afternoon/evening.*

see you ...

Hasta **luego.** *See you.* lit. *Until then.*
Hasta **mañana.** *See you tomorrow.*
Hasta **pronto.** *See you soon.*
Nos vemos **en Valencia.** *See you in Valencia.*
Nos vemos **el lunes.** *See you on Monday.*
Nos vemos **más tarde.** *See you later.*
Vale. *OK.*
Venga; hasta luego, chico/chica. *OK; bye/see you, mate.*

terms of endearment

Spanish terms of affection include **cariño** (for male and female) and **querido/querida** (m/f), which are the equivalent of *darling.* You'll also hear, or be called, **mi amor** or, in Latin America, **amor mío** or **corazoncito.** They all mean *love.*

Chico and **chica** are commonly used to greet friends, as is **hombre** (lit. *man*) when you bump into an acquaintance unexpectedly. Don't be surprised if someone greets you with the words ¿**Qué tal, hija?** or **Hola hijo, ¿qué tal?** It doesn't mean they literally think you're their daughter (**hija**) or son (**hijo**), it's just a friendly greeting.

In Latin America, physical attributes are sometimes used as affectionate ways of addressing friends: ¿**Qué tal, flaquito?** *How are you, skinny?* **Hola rubita** *Hi blondie* **Oye, gordito** *Hey, chubby.*

meeting people

When meeting for the first time, men tend to shake hands and women exchange one or two kisses. A man and a woman usually shake hands; as friends, they will generally exchange kisses. When younger people meet or are introduced, they tend to exchange kisses as a matter of course. Spanish culture is generally more touchy-feely than the UK's.

The key words for introductions come from the verb **ser** *to be*.

yo	soy	*I am*	**nosotros/as**	somos	*we are*
tú	eres	*you are*	**vosotros/as**	sois	*you are*
usted	es	*you are*	**ustedes**	son	*you are*
él/ella	es	*he/she is*	**ellos/ellas**	son	*they are*
	es	*it is*			

The words in blue are the important ones. **Yo, tú, usted**, etc. are used much less than in English, although they are needed if there's a risk of confusion or for emphasis: **Ella es inglesa, pero yo soy escocés.** *She's English but I'm Scottish.*

I'm not is **no soy**, and the others work in the same way: **no es** *he/she's not*.

(Yo) soy **Jon.** *I'm Jon.*
Soy **inglés/irlandés.** *I'm English/Irish.*
Soy **de Exeter.** *I'm from Exeter.*

Me llamo Meg Riley. *My name's Meg Riley.*
Mi nombre es Meg Riley. *My name's Meg Riley.*
Mi apellido es Riley. *My surname is Riley.*

To confirm who you're talking to, you use the correct part of **ser**. Spanish speakers will usually add **¿no?** or **¿verdad?** *aren't you?* to the question.
¿Sois vosotros la familia MacLeod? *Are you the MacLeods?*
Tú eres Miguel, ¿no? *Are you Miguel? You're Miguel, aren't you?*
Usted es María Méndez, ¿verdad? *María Méndez, I believe?*

Mucho gusto. *Good to meet you.* (male or female speaking)
Encantado. *Delighted to meet you.* (male speaking)
Encantada. *Delighted to meet you.* (female speaking)
Es un placer conocerte/le. *It's a pleasure to meet you.* **(tú/usted)**
A sus órdenes. *At your service.* (used in Latin America)

spelling names

You might be asked how you spell your name or want to know how someone else spells theirs. The key question is **¿Cómo se escribe?** *How do you write it?*, literally *How is it written?*

If you're speaking face to face, you can just say **Se escribe ...** *It's written ...* and write it down. Otherwise, on the phone for instance, you'll need to spell it out using the names of the letters in the Spanish alphabet, which sound like this:

a **a** *ah*	b **be** *beh*	c **ce** *theh*
d **de** *deh*	e **e** *eh*	f **efe** *ehfeh*
g **ge** *heh*	h **hache** *ahcheh*	i **i** *ee*
j **jota** *hota*	k **ka** *kah*	l **ele** *ehleh*
m **eme** *ehmeh*	n **ene** *ehneh*	ñ **eñe** *ehnyeh*
o **o** *oh*	p **pe** *peh*	q **cu** *koo*
r **erre** *ehreh*	s **ese** *ehseh*	t **te** *teh*
u **u** *oo*	v **uve** *oobeh*	w **uve doble** *oobeh dohbleh*
x **equis** *ehkees*	y **i griega** *ee gree ehgah*	z **zeta** *thehtah*

Double letters are signalled with the word **doble**: *double c* is **ce doble**. However, **ll**, which used to be included as a separate letter in the Spanish alphabet, has its own name: **elle**, which is pronounced *ehlieh*.

With letters that might be confused, such as **b** and **p**, people will often refer to a country or well-known city to clarify the spelling: **¿P de Pamplona? No, b de Barcelona**.

Me llamo Carol Kerry. Kerry se escribe ka, e, erre doble, i griega *My name's Carol Kerry. Kerry is spelt ...*
Mi nombre es Sofía – con efe de Francia. *My name's Sofía —with f for France.*
Mi apellido es López. Se escribe ele, o, p de Pamplona, e, zeta. *My surname is López. It's written l, o, p for Pamplona, e, z.*
Mi nombre es Michael. Se escribe eme, i, ce, hache, a, e, ele. Pero todos me llaman Mick, como Mick Jagger. *My name's Michael. It's written ... But everyone calls me Mick, like Mick Jagger.*

> It's well worth working out how to spell out your own name in Spanish and committing it to memory.

introductions

There are two ways of introducing someone. The first is **este es/esta es** *this is*. You might have come across these written **éste** and **ésta**, but in 2010 new guidelines on Spanish spelling proposed a number of changes, including removing the accents from them.

Este es mi colega, Jack. *This is my colleague, Jack.*

Esta es mi hermana pequeña/mi hermanita, Federica. *This is my little sister, Federica.*

Este es mi hermano menor/mayor. *This is my younger/older brother.*

Esta es mi mejor amiga, Marta. *This is my best friend, Marta.*

Estos son mis hermanos, Jorge y David. *These are my brothers, Jorge and David.*

Esta es mi tía Julia, la hermana de mi madre. *This is my Aunt Julia, my mother's sister.*

In Spanish, there's no equivalent of the English apostrophe s. Instead of *my sister's ex-husband*, you say *the ex-husband of my sister*.

Este es el exmarido de mi hermana. *This is my sister's ex-husband.*

Estas son las amigas de mi novia. *These are my fiancée's (girl)friends.*

More formally, you can use **Te presento a** ..., which literally means *To you I introduce* ... When *you* is **usted**, you need **Le presento a** ..., for **vosotros/as** it's **Os presento a** ... and for **ustedes** it's **Les presento a** ...

Te presento a Juan. *Let me introduce Juan (to you).*
Le presento a mi tío y a mi tía. *Let me introduce my uncle and my aunt.*
Os presento a mi amigo, Pepe. *Let me introduce my friend, Pepe.*
Te presento a mis hermanas. *Let me introduce my sisters.*
Les presento a mi colega, Sofía. *Let me introduce my colleague, Sofía.*
Te presento a Cristóbal: somos amigos de la infancia. *Let me introduce Cristóbal: we're childhood friends.*
Le presento a Manuela, mi novia/pareja. *Let me introduce my girlfriend/ partner, Manuela.*
Os presento a Rogelio, el novio/la pareja de mi hijo. *Let me introduce Rogelio, my son's boyfriend/partner.*
Le presento a mis colegas. *Let me introduce my colleagues (to you).*
Os presento a mis padres. *Let me introduce my parents.*
Te presento a mis abuelos. *Let me introduce my grandparents.*

The **a** after **te/le/os/les presento** is a distinctive feature of Spanish, called the personal **a**. It's included when the direct object of a verb is a specific person or a pet, and it's not translated in English.

¿Conoces a María? *Do you know María?*
Queremos a nuestro gato. *We love our cat.*
Voy a ver a mi abuela. *I'm going to see my grandmother.*

But, **Quiero ver la última película de Almodóvar** *I want to see Almodóvar's latest film.*

Practise introductions. Imagine you want to introduce members of your family and circle of friends. It's much more effective if you do this out loud rather than in your head. When you've finished, write down two or three of your introductions.

Remember that mi is **my** *when you're introducing one person, and mis for more than one. Make sure you match este and esta to the right genders and use estos or estas for more than one person.*

basic courtesies

Perdone means *Excuse me*. To a friend, you'd say **Perdona**. This, or **¿Me permite?**, is also the expression to use if you need to get past someone, although **Con permiso** is commonly used in Latin America. To attract someone's attention, a waiter for example, use **Perdón** or **Por favor**.

Por favor means *please*. Spaniards don't tend to use *please* as much as English speakers do. This is because it's often implicit in the tone of a sentence.

Gracias. *Thank you.*
Muchas gracias. *Thank you very much.*
Mil gracias. *Thank you so much.*

A response such as **De nada** *You're welcome* or **No hay de qué** *Think nothing of it* is expected in response to **Gracias**.

¿Puedo? *May I?* is how to ask if it's OK to do something, such as take a chair in a café or open a window, when it's obvious from the context what you're referring to.
The answer is usually **Por supuesto, claro** *Of course. Do.*

Perdone is also used to say *sorry* for bumping into someone. For a proper apology, you need **Lo siento** or **Disculpe** *I'm sorry*. The response is usually **No pasa nada** or **Nada, hombre** *No problem*.

To welcome someone, you use **bienvenido** or **bienvenida**, depending on whether the guest is male or female. **Bienvenidos/as** is used for more than one person, and if they're a mixed group, it's **bienvenidos**.

You can make people feel at home and comfortable with:

tú	**Estás en tu casa.**	
usted	**Está en su casa.**	*Make yourself at home.*
vosotros/as	**Estáis en vuestra casa.**	
ustedes	**Están en su casa.**	

When you're eating with other people, it's customary to wish everyone **¡Que aproveche!** *Enjoy your meal.*

talking the talk

The **Talking the Talk** page towards the end of each chapter sets out the transcript of the informal conversations on the audio.

Listen to the conversation first – at least a couple of times – before you read it here. Assuming that you have worked through the chapter, you'll probably be able to get the gist and pick out some details. At the same time you'll be getting familiar with the rhythm of Spanish. You'll find practical ideas in your **Audio Support Pack** on how to make the most of these conversations.

Isabel	¡Javier! Hola. ¿Qué tal?
Javier	Vamos tirando, ¿y tú?
Isabel	¡Genial, gracias! ¡Papá! ... Javier, te presento a mi padre, Jorge ... y esta es mi tía Loli.
Javier	Mucho gusto señor, señora.
Jorge	Encantado.
Loli	Encantada.
Isabel	Mi tía es la hermana de mi madre.
Javier	¿Cómo se llama?
Isabel	Dolores ..., pero todos la llaman Loli.
Isabel	Este es mi hermano, Ángel ... y su novia, Daniela.
Javier	Mucho gusto.
Isabel	... y esta es mi mejor amiga, Lucía.
Javier	Hola, ¿qué tal, Lucía?
Isabel	... Sophie es una amiga inglesa.
Javier	Hola. Sophie es como Sofía, ¿no?
Sophie	Sí, pero se escribe ese, o, pe, hache, i, e.
Javier	Venga ... pues, nos vemos mañana.
Isabel	Adiós, Javier. ¡Hasta mañana!
Sophie	¡Adiós!

checkpoint 1

1   What would you say when trying to make your way out of a crowded lift?

2   Would you use **tú, usted** or **vosotros/as** when speaking to a close friend's elderly grandmother?

3   When being introduced to a woman, does a man say **Encantado** or **Encantada**? If you're introducing a colleague to a couple of Spanish friends, do you say **Les presento a mi colega** or **Os presento a mi colega**?

4   To introduce yourself, what word do you say before your name? How do you make that word negative?

5   If you're addressing a man who you haven't met before, which of these is the safest word to use: **hombre, amigo** or **señor**?

6   What could you add to **Gracias** to say *Thank you very much*? Give two ways in which you might respond to **Gracias**.

7   If someone replied to your **¿Cómo estás?** with **¡Fatal!**, would it be more appropriate to commiserate or give them a high five?

8   What's the Spanish for *Welcome!* when talking to more than one person?

9   What's the Spanish for *See you tomorrow, See you soon, See you later*?

10 What word is missing from **¿Conoces ... mi amigo, Jorge?**

11 What's the difference between **soy, son** and **somos**?

12 At what time of day do you use **Buenas tardes**?

13 Which of these relatives is definitely younger than you: **hija, tía, madre, primo, abuelo**?

14 How would you invite a couple to make themselves at home?

15 What's the word for surname? Spell out yours to someone.

16 What words are missing from these introductions? **Esta es mi .... María, la hermana de mi madre. .... es Peter, mi hermano.**

17 Someone accidentally bumps into you. How would you respond to their **¡Perdone!**?

18 You're checking that this is the person you're supposed to meet. In what two ways could you complete **Usted es la señora Reyes, ¿ .... ?**

19 How would you suggest that **tú** should be used instead of **usted**?

20 What single word would you use to ask if you can sit at this café table?

dos
getting to know people

The stereotyped view of Spaniards as extremely sociable and approachable is borne out in reality. You'll find that people are genuinely interested in your personal and family life and very comfortable discussing them.

Getting to know people implies that you'll be telling them about yourself, so it's worth becoming thoroughly familiar with the words you need to do this, as well as practising some complete sentences.

But, of course, a good conversation is a two-way process which involves asking as well as answering questions. Closed questions such as *Do you work here?* or *Have you been to London?* can result in a simple yes or no. Open questions, on the other hand, elicit more information; this type of question uses words such as **¿dónde?** *where?*, **¿cuándo?** *when?*, **¿por qué?** *why?* An unusual feature of written Spanish is the upside down question mark at the beginning of questions. The same goes for exclamation marks.

You'll probably need to establish early on that you're keen to speak Spanish, as you'll find that people may be equally keen to practise their English on you.
¿Te/Le/Os/Les importa si hablo español? *Do you mind if I speak in Spanish?*
Estoy aprendiendo español/Aprendo español. *I'm learning Spanish.*
Estoy estudiando español. *I'm studying Spanish*
Quiero practicar un poco. *I'd like to practise a bit.*

asking questions

Ice-breakers and chat-up lines, which are the same the world over, usually involve a question:

¿Está aquí de negocios o de vacaciones? *Are you here on business or on holiday?* **(usted)**
¿Es la primera vez que estás aquí? *Is this the first time you've been here?* **(tú)**
¿Llevas/Lleva mucho tiempo aquí? *Have you been here long?*
Es un sitio precioso/hermoso, ¿verdad? *Isn't this a beautiful place?*

The simplest way to ask a question in Spanish is to raise the pitch of your voice at the end of a statement: **Estás de vacaciones** *You are on holiday;* **¿Estás de vacaciones?** *Are you on holiday?*

You can also ask a question by adding ¿**no**? or ¿**verdad**? to a statement. They're the equivalent of English question tags such as *isn't it, is he/she, don't we, aren't you, have you, won't they?*

Trabajas aquí, ¿no? *You work here, don't you?*
No trabajas aquí, ¿verdad? *You don't work here, do you?*
Es el guía, ¿no? *That's the guide, right?*

When using a question word like ¿**cuándo**?, the verb goes straight after it, without extra words like *do/does/did*: ¿**Cuándo llega?** *When does he/she arrive? When is he/she arriving?*
As in English, the question words start the sentence, unless there's a word like **para, con** or **de**: ¿**Para quién es?** *Who is it for?*

¿**quién**? ¿**quiénes**? *who?*
¿**Quién es el director ejecutivo?** *Who's the CEO?*
¿**Quién es?** *Who's there? e.g. when answering an entryphone*
¿**Con** quién **viajas?** *Who are you travelling with?*
¿**Quiénes son aquellas personas?** *Who are those people?*

¿**qué**? *what?*
¿**Qué quiere?** *What do you want?*
¿**Qué pasa?** *What's the matter? What's happening? What's up?*
¿**Qué vamos a hacer?** *What shall we do?*
¿**Para qué es esto?** *What's this for?*

¿**cómo**? *how?* or sometimes *what?*
¿**Cómo estás?** *How are you?*
¿**Cómo se dice ... en español?** *How do you say ... in Spanish?*
¿**Cómo se llama tu hermano?** *What's your brother called?*

¿dónde? *where?* ¿de dónde? *from where?* ¿adónde? *to where?*
¿De dónde **eres?** ¿De dónde **es?** *Where are you from?*
¿Dónde **naciste?** *Where were you born?* **(tú)**
¿Adónde **quieres ir esta tarde?** *Where do you want to go (to) this evening?*
(tú)

¿cuándo? *when?*
¿Cuándo **es tu cumpleaños?** *When's your birthday?*
¿Cuándo **os casasteis?** *When did you two get married?* **(vosotros)**
¿Hasta cuándo **estás en España?** *Until when are you in Spain?* **(tú)**

¿por qué? *why?*
¿Por qué **te/le gusta esta región?** *Why do you like this region?*
¿Por qué **no ha venido tu novio?** *Why hasn't your boyfriend come?*
¿Por qué **no?** *Why not?*

¿cuál? ¿cuáles? *which? what? which ones?*
¿Cuál **es tu correo electrónico?** *What's your email address?*
¿Cuál **es tu nombre?** *What's your name?*
¿Cuál **es tu plato preferido?** *Which/What is your favourite dish?*
¿Cuáles **son las diferencias entre los dos?** *What are the differences between the two?*

¿qué? or ¿cuál?
Both can mean *what?* and the difference is quite subtle.
Qué is used when the answer is completely unrestricted:
¿Qué **es eso?** *What is that?* ¿Qué **quieres?** *What do you want?*
Cuál is used to select from a limited number of possibilities:
¿Cuál **es tu nombre?** *What's your name?* (from the range of possible names)
¿Cuál **prefieres, la grande o la pequeña?** *Which do you prefer, the big one or the small one?*

¿cuánto? ¿cuánta? *How much?*
¿Cuánto **pesa?** *How much does it weigh?*
¿Cuánto **cuesta una entrada?** *How much does a ticket cost?*
¿Cuánta **harina necesitas para este pastel?** *How much flour do you need for this cake?*

¿cuántos? ¿cuántas? *how many?*
¿Cuántos **años tienes?** *How old are you?* lit. *How many years do you have?*
¿Cuántos **hijos tenéis?** *How many children do you (both) have?*
¿Cuántas **habitaciones hay?** *How many rooms are there?*

sharing information

As you get to know people, the more information you tend to share and the more detail you get into. This usually entails descriptions, for which you need adjectives.

Spanish adjectives are listed in dictionaries with their masculine singular ending. This is very often **-o**, which changes to **-a** (not only when talking about females but also any feminine noun). Adjectives that end in **-e** or **-es** are the same for masculine and feminine.

Several adjectives describing nationality end in **-és**, which becomes **-esa** in the feminine (e.g. **francés > francesa** French), while a word ending in -l, like **español** Spanish, adds -a (**española**).

In the plural, you simply add **-s** to the masculine or feminine adjective, except for those ending in a consonant, which insert **e** before the **-s**: **españoles, españolas.**

Soy ... *I'm ...*

americano/a *American*	**argentino/a** *Argentinian*
australiano/a *Australian*	**boliviano/a** *Bolivian*
canadiense *Canadian*	**chileno/a** *Chilean*
galés/esa *Welsh*	**colombiano/a** *Colombian*
inglés/esa *English*	**costarricense** *Costa Rican*
irlandés/esa *Irish*	**peruano/a** *Peruvian*
escocés/esa *Scottish*	**venezolano/a** *Venezuelan*

To talk about other people, you use **es** *is*, **son** *are*, **era** *was*, **eran** *were*:

Mi madre es escocesa. *My mother is Scottish.*
Mi bisabuelo era irlandés. *My great-grandfather was Irish.*
Nuestra nuera es polaca. *Our daughter-in-law is Polish.*
Mi exmujer es galesa. *My ex-wife is Welsh.*
Mis suegros son americanos. *My in-laws are American.*
Su madre es argentina, pero su padre era español, de Galicia.
Her mother is Argentinian but her father was Spanish, from Galicia.
Soy australiano, pero mi padre es inglés. *I'm Australian but my father is English.*
Tu abuelo era boliviano, ¿no? *Your grandfather was Bolivian, wasn't he?*

ser and estar *to be*

Spanish has two verbs for talking about being: **ser** and **estar**.

Ser (page 18) is generally used to say what is permanent and unchanging, like one's nationality, or to talk about something that changes very slowly, such as being young or old.

Estar tends to describe more transient things like moods or states: **Estoy contento** *I'm happy*, **Está viva** *She's alive*, **La tienda** está **abierta** *The shop is open*. It's also used for location and position: **Está en la cocina** *It's in the kitchen.*

yo	estoy	*I am*	**nosotros/as**	estamos	*we are*
tú	estás	*you are*	**vosotros/as**	estáis	*you are*
usted	está	*you are*	**ustedes**	están	*you are*
él/ella	está	*he/she is*	**ellos/ellas**	están	*they are*
	está	*it is*			

soy
hetero(sexual) *straight*
homosexual *homosexual*
gay *gay* (plural **gais**)
lesbiana *lesbian*
bisexual *bisexual*
transexual *transexual*
transgénero/a *transgender*
pareja de hecho *in a civil partnership*

estoy
soltero/a *single*
casado/a *married*
... por la iglesia *in a religious ceremony*
... por lo civil *in a civil ceremony*
separado/a *separated*
divorciado/a *divorced*
prometido/a *engaged*
viudo/a *widowed*

Estar is the one to use when talking about how you are and how you're feeling.
¿Cómo estás/está/estáis/están? *How are you?*
Estoy bien, gracias. *I'm fine, thanks.*
No estoy bien. *I'm not well.*

Take care not to confuse **casado/a** *married* with **cansado/a** *tired*!

tener *to have, to own*

Tener is one of the most used verbs in Spanish. Its basic meaning is *to have* but it also has other uses where the word *have* doesn't feature in the English.

yo	tengo	*I have (got)*	**nosotros/as**	tenemos	*we have*
tú	tienes	*you have*	**vosotros/as**	tenéis	*you have*
usted	tiene	*you have*	**ustedes**	tienen	*you have*
él/ella	tiene	*he/she has*	**ellos/ellas**	tienen	*they have*
	tiene	*it has*			

It's used in the widest sense of *to have, to own, to possess*:
Tengo dos entradas para esta tarde. *I've got two tickets for this evening.*
Tiene los ojos azules. *She has blue eyes.*
Tenemos dos perros y un gato. *We have two dogs and a cat.*
Tengo pareja. *I'm in a relationship. lit. I have a partner.*

It's used to talk about family.
¿Tienes hijos? *Do you have children?*
¿Cuántos hermanos tienes? *How many brothers and sisters do you have?*

Tengo/Tenemos ... *I/we have ...*
 ... un hermano, una hermana. *... a/one brother, sister.*
 ... un hijo/una hija. *... a son/a daughter.*
 ... dos hijas adoptadas. *... two adopted daughters.*
 ... tres hijos adultos. *... three grown-up children.*
 ... seis nietos: dos nietas y cuatro nietos. *... six grandchildren: two granddaughters and four grandsons.*
No tengo/tenemos hijos. *I/we don't have children.*

It's used to talk about age, literally translated as *to have ... years*:
¿Cuántos años tienes? *How old are you?*
Tengo quince años. *I'm 15.*

Mi madre tiene sesenta años. *My mother is 60.*

¿Cuántos años tiene el niño? *How old is the little boy?*
Tiene tres años. *He's three years old.* **Parece más mayor.** *He looks older.*

Tener is also used to talk about health.

Tengo ... *I have .../***Tiene ...** *He/she has ...*
    ... dolor de cabeza. *... a headache.*
    ... dolor de garganta. *... a sore throat.*
    ... dolor de estómago. *... stomach ache.*
    ... dolor de espalda. *... backache.*
    ... un resfriado. *... a cold.*
    ... gripe. *... flu.*
    ... fiebre. *... a temperature.*
    ... alergia al polen. *... hayfever.*
    ... diarrea. *... diarrhoea.*
    ... un dolor en el pecho. *... a pain in the chest.*
    ... quemaduras de sol. *... sunburn.*
    ... una insolación. *... sunstroke.*
    ... resaca. *... a hangover.*
    ... mareos. *I feel dizzy.*
    ... náuseas. *I feel sick.*

Tengo **diabetes.** *I'm diabetic.*
Tengo alergia al **trigo/a los productos lácteos.** *I'm allergic to wheat/dairy products.*
No sé lo que tengo/tiene. *I don't know what's wrong with me/with him/her.*

Spanish often uses **tener** + noun where English uses *to be* + adjective:
    tener hambre *to be hungry*
    tener sed *to be thirsty*
    tener miedo *to be afraid*
    tener razón *to be right*
    tener sueño *to be sleepy*
    tener prisa *to be in a hurry*
    tener calor *to be hot*
    tener frío *to be cold*

Yo no tengo miedo. *I'm not scared.*
Tú tienes razón. *You're right.*
Tengo **mucha** sed. *I'm incredibly thirsty.*
¿Tienes **demasiado** calor/frío? *Are you too hot/cold?*
Tengo sueño; **necesito irme a la cama.** *I'm sleepy; I need my bed.*

People also commonly say **Me muero de hambre/sed/frío/calor** to say *I'm dying of hunger/thirst/cold/heat.*

describing people

You ask what people are like with ¿cómo?

¿Cómo es **Jaime?**/¿Cómo es **Isabel?** *What's Jaime/Isabel like?*
¿Cómo es **su media naranja?** *What's your other half like?*
¿Cómo son **tus vecinos/colegas?** *What are your neighbours/colleagues like?*

You describe someone's character or personality with **ser** and adjectives:
Jaime es amable y atento. *Jaime's kind and thoughtful.*
Irene es simpática. *Irene's nice.*
Los gemelos son tímidos. *The twins are shy.*
Mis colegas son competentes. *My colleagues are competent.*

When talking about what someone looks like, there's no precise Spanish equivalent of the word *look*. To describe the colour of eyes or hair, you use the verb **tener** followed by an unexpected **el, la** or **los.**

¿Cómo es físicamente? *What does he/she look like?*
¿Qué aspecto tiene? *What does he/she look like?*
Es alto. Mide dos metros ... *He's tall. He's 2 metres tall ...*
... mientras que ella es baja, mide un metro sesenta. *... while she's short, 1 metre 60.*
Pesa setenta kilos, más o menos. *He/she weighs about 70 kilos.*
Tiene los ojos marrones/azules. *He/she has brown/blue eyes.*
Tiene el pelo largo/corto/rizado/liso. *He/she has long/short/curly/straight hair.*

You can bring your descriptions to life by:

● adding **muy** *very*, **poco** *not very*, **bastante** *quite*, **algo** *rather*, **un poco** *a bit*, **super** *really*, **tan** *so*. They don't change.

or

● replacing the final vowel of many adjectives with **-ísimo/a**, which has to agree with what it's describing, e.g. **altísimo/a** *very tall, extremely tall.*

Es muy simpática. *She's very nice.*
Los gemelos son algo tímidos. *The twins are rather shy.*
Tiene el pelo larguísimo/cortísimo. *She has really long/short hair.*
Sois tan generosos. *You're (both) so generous.*
Lo que hacen es tan irresponsable. *What they're doing is so irresponsible.*
El camarero es superguapo, ¿no? *The waiter's really good-looking, isn't he?*

wordbank

physical descriptions

alto *tall*
atractivo *attractive, good-looking*
bajo *short*
calvo *bald*
delgado *slim*
feo *ugly*
flaco *thin, skinny*
fuerte *strong, strongly built*

gordo *fat*
guapo *beautiful, handsome*
moreno *dark*
musculoso *muscular*
pelirrojo *ginger*
rollizo *plump*
robusto *solid, burly*
rubio *blonde*

character and personality

abierto *open, friendly*
agresivo *aggressive*
alegre *happy, cheerful*
amable *kind*
antipático *nasty, mean*
artístico *artistic*
astuto *canny, shrewd*
atrevido *bold, brazen*
capaz *able, competent*
cariñoso *affectionate*
descarado *cheeky*
desconsiderado *inconsiderate*
descuidado *scruffy*
trabajador *hard-working*
discreto *tactful, diplomatic*
dotado *gifted*
educado *polite*
egoísta *selfish*
exigente *demanding*
fiable *reliable, trustworthy*
fiel *faithful, loyal*
generoso *generous, kind-hearted*

hábil *capable, talented*
indiscreto *indiscreet, tactless*
ingenuo *naive*
impetuoso *rash, impetuous*
irresponsable *irresponsible*
listo *clever*
maleducado *rude*
nervioso *anxious*
optimista *optimistic*
paciente *patient*
pesimista *pessimistic*
perezoso *lazy*
prudente *cautious, prudent*
relajado *laid-back*
religioso *religious*
seguro (de sí mismo) *confident*
sensible *sensitive*
sereno *placid*
simpático *nice*
sin pelos en la lengua *outspoken*
terco *stubborn*
tonto *dumb, stupid*

Try describing a neighbour, a member of your family and a celebrity of some kind (male and female). Use as many suitable adjectives as you can, both flattering and negative. Make a point of using extras such as *muy* and *algo*. Try adding -*ísimo/a* to at least one adjective.

where you're living or staying

Vivir means *to live.*
¿Dónde vives/vive/vivís/viven? *Where do you live?*
¿Dónde (exactamente) en España? *Whereabouts (exactly) in Spain?*
Vivimos en Valencia/en una casa moderna/cerca de la estación.
We live in Valencia/in a modern house/near the station.

To find out where someone is staying, you ask **¿Dónde te alojas?** or **¿Dónde te quedas?**
¿Dónde te alojas/se aloja/os alojáis/se alojan? *Where are you staying?*
¿Os quedáis en un hotel/en un apartamento? *Are you staying in a hotel/an apartment?*

You can ask for more detail with **¿Es ...?** or with phrases like **¿Dónde está?** and **¿Cómo es?**
¿Es grande, la ciudad? *Is it a big town/city?*
¿Cómo es el paisaje? *What's the landscape like?*
¿Cómo es la región? *What's the region like?*
¿Cómo es el pueblo/la ciudad/el hotel? *What's the village/town/hotel like?*
¿Dónde está el camping? *Where's the campsite?*

Hay means *there is* or *there are* and, as a question, *is there?* or *are there?*:
¿Hay una piscina/una cancha de tenis? *Is there a pool/a tennis court?*
¿Hay un parque infantil? *Is there a children's play area?*
¿Qué servicios hay? *What services/facilities are there?*
Hay un bar, pero no hay restaurante. *There's a bar but there isn't a restaurant.*

When talking about where a place is situated, you can also use **se encuentra**, although **¿dónde está?** is the simplest way to ask where something is.

Mi pueblo/El pueblo donde vivo se encuentra entre Cambridge y Londres.
The town where I live is between Cambridge and London.
Es un lugar ... *The place is ...*
    ... grande/bastante pequeño. *... big/quite small.*
    ... concurrido/tranquilo. *... crowded/tranquil.*
    ... en alza. *... up and coming.*

La zona donde vivimos está ... *The area we live in is ...*
      ... en el noreste del Reino Unido. ... *in the north-east of the UK.*
      ... en Cornualles/en la parte oeste de Yorkshire. ... *in Cornwall/in West Yorkshire.*

es or está?

Es is used with an adjective to describe something that is a lasting quality, inherent or unlikely to change. **Es acogedor/barato/muy caro.** *It's welcoming/cheap/very expensive.*

Está on the other hand describes something that is more temporary and could therefore change. **Está muy sucio** *It's very dirty* (but could become **limpio** *clean* if someone made an effort to change the situation).

El hotel ... *The hotel ...*
      ... es pequeño, céntrico y barato. ... *is small, central and cheap.*
      ... está bien equipado. ... *is well-equipped.*
      ... está bien cuidado/algo deteriorado. ... *is well-kept/somewhat run-down.*
      ... está en primera línea de playa. ... *is on the seafront.*

El campamento/el centro turístico ... *The campsite/resort ...*
      ... es de primera categoría. ... *is categorised as first class.*
      ... está a la sombra/al sol. ... *is shaded/sunny.*
      ... está a cien metros de la playa. ... *is 100 metres from the beach.*

Hay mucho que hacer. *There's plenty to do.*
Hay un campo de deportes y mesas de pimpón. *There's a playing field and table-tennis tables.*

Un campo means *a field* as in **campo de deportes** *playing field*, **campo de fútbol** *football field* and also **campo de actividad** *field of activity*. **Campo de golf** is a *golf course*. But **campo** also has the meaning of *countryside*: **casa de campo** *country house*, **ir al campo** *to go to the country*.

word bank

chiquito *tiny*, **pequeño** *small*, **estrecho** *narrow, cramped*
grande *big*, **enorme** *huge*, **ancho** *wide*
cómodo *comfortable*, **abierto** *open*, **espacioso** *spacious*

nuevo *new*, **viejo** *old*
moderno *modern*, **antiguo** *ancient*, **histórico** *historic*
anticuado *dated*, **deteriorado** *dilapidated*
sencillo *simple, basic*, **lujoso** *luxurious*

tranquilo *quiet*, **concurrido** *crowded, busy*
animado *lively, bustling*, **congestionado** *congested*

rústico *rustic*, **lejano** *remote*
boscoso *wooded*, **montañoso** *mountainous*
accidentado *rugged, rough*, **empinado** *steep*, **llano** *flat*
pedregoso *rocky, stony*

urbano *urban*
industrial *industrial*, **céntrico** *central*, **turístico** *touristy*

soleado *sunny*, **árido** *dry*, **embarrado** *muddy*
arenoso *sandy*

limpio *clean*, **inmaculado** *immaculate*
bien equipado *well-equipped*, **bien cuidado** *well-kept*
sucio *dirty*, **contaminado** *polluted*, **descuidado** *neglected*

encantador *fascinating, charming*, **puro** *pure, unspoilt*, **bonito** *lovely, beautiful*, **magnífico** *superb*, **grandioso** *imposing*, **pintoresco** *picturesque*
ruidoso *noisy*, **deprimente** *dismal, depressing*

how to remember words

It's all very well having a bank of words to refer to — but how do you remember them?

The key to transferring a word to your long-term memory is to consciously *do something with it.* What you do depends on how you personally learn best — try some of these suggestions and see which suit you.

Don't try and learn too many words at the same time. Aim for a group of seven or eight: it helps if there's some connection between them.

- Listen to the words online. If you enter into most search engines the words *luxurious in Spanish* or *translate into Spanish luxurious,* the first result will be **lujoso**. Click on the speaker icon and listen to how it's said — as many times as you want. Try it with *dirty to* hear how the Spanish sounds.

- Say the words out loud — several times. Some people swear by doing this last thing at night, then again the next morning.

- Others remember the way words look on a page. If you have a visual memory, the unusual arrangement of the words opposite should help you. If so, use a similar technique when you make your own notes.

- Don't always think in individual words. Sometimes a pair or a group of words can be more memorable, e.g. **algo deteriorado** or **Es pequeño, céntrico y barato**.

- Write words down. It doesn't matter whether you write them on paper or key them in. Keep them in manageable groups rather than an endless list. Highlight words that you think will be the most useful (but don't discount others since you never know what someone is going to say to you).

- Learn tricky words first. You're going to remember words like **moderno**, **rural** or **región** anyway, so leave them until last.

- Use associations to help you remember words. For example, the Spanish for *rugged* or *rough* is **accidentado**, so think of stumbling along a rough track and having an accident.

- *Use* the words. Use the ones opposite as suggested, but don't stop there. Whenever you're out and about, think of an adjective to describe the places you see. It could be factual: **pequeño, viejo, deteriorado**; or it could be subjective: **encantador, deprimente**.

talking the talk

Javier	Es un lugar espectacular, ¿verdad?
Tourist	Sí, es superbonito.
Javier	No trabajas aquí, ¿verdad? ¿Estás de vacaciones?
Tourist	Sí. Estoy de vacaciones con dos amigas.
Javier	¿De dónde sois?
Tourist	De Bristol; somos todas inglesas.
Javier	Pero hablas muy bien español.
Tourist	Gracias ... mi abuela era colombiana.
Javier	¡Ah! ¡Que lo paséis muy bien!
Tourist	¿Perdone?
Javier	¡Que lo paséis muy bien!
Tourist	Muchas gracias.
Isabel	Sophie es simpática, ¿verdad?
Javier	Muy simpática. Habla bien español ... y es muy atractiva.
Isabel	Pero es algo ingenua.
Javier	¿Cuántos años tiene?
Isabel	¿Sophie? ... Veinticinco ... o veintiséis. ¿Y tú, Javier? No eres de aquí. ¿De dónde eres?
Javier	Bueno, soy de un pueblo que se llama Medina de Rioseco.
Isabel	¿Dónde está exactamente?
Javier	Se encuentra en la comunidad de Castilla y León, en el norte de España, cerca de la ciudad de Valladolid.
Isabel	¿Y cómo es Medina de Rioseco?
Javier	Es bastante pequeño, es histórico. Tiene un castillo muy antiguo que está en ruinas.
Isabel	¿Tu familia vive en Medina de Rioseco?
Javier	Sí.
Isabel	¿Tienes mucha familia? ¿Tienes hermanos?
Javier	Tengo una hermana y un hermano.

verb practice 1

1 Fill the gaps with the correct forms of **ser** or **estar** *to be* (pages 18 and 29) and say what the sentences mean.

a Yo .... divorciado.

b Nosotros no .... ingleses.

c Cristina .... muy simpática.

d Él y su hermano .... gemelos.

e ¿Hasta cuándo .... vosotros aquí?

f El hostal .... limpio.

g Yo no .... muy religioso.

h El señor Campos .... calvo.

i Ellos .... muy simpáticos.

j Tú .... venezolana, ¿no?

2 Now do the same using **tener** *to have.*

a Yo .... ojos azules, pero mi hija .... ojos marrones.

b Paco no .... sueño.

c ¿Cuántos años .... Mariluz?

d Mi mujer y yo .... gripe.

e ¿ .... tú dieciocho o diecinueve años?

f Vosotros .... tres hijos, ¿verdad?

g Ellos .... una pequeña casa en centro ciudad.

h ¿Usted .... hambre, señora?

3 How would you ask these questions in Spanish?

a *Is she Canadian or American?*

b *Are Marta and Conchi sisters?*

c *Does the hotel have a pool?*

d *Pablo's gay, isn't he?*

e *Are you thirsty?* (**tú, usted, vosotros/as** and **ustedes**)

f *Are there tennis courts?*

 Jot down a few lines about yourself. Include all the information you can but keep it structurally simple. Use soy + your nationality and what you look like, and estar + your relationship status; use tengo and no tengo with at least five nouns, e.g. siblings, children, pets, house; and vivo + where you live.

Now make a list of the questions you would need to ask to get this information from other people.

checkpoint 2

1   How do you tell people you're learning Spanish?

2   *Isn't it, is she, aren't you, didn't we* at the end of a question can all be expressed by which two words in Spanish?

3   Which part of **vivir** should be used here? **Mi hija y su novio .... en las afueras** (*outskirts*) **de Madrid.**

4   Name in Spanish three recreational facilities you might expect to find in a holiday complex.

5   **Dónde, por qué, cuál, cuántos, qué, quién, cuánto, cuándo, cómo.** Rearrange these question words into the order *who, which, why, what, when, where, how, how many, how much.*

6   How would you ask a couple what their names are?

7   Work out the Spanish for: *I'm not thirsty, Are you cold?* (**tú**)*, She's right, I'm not in a hurry today.*

8   Add the correct ending to these adjectives and translate the sentences: **Mi abuelo está viud_, Mis amigos son gales_, Mi prima es rubi_, Mi vecina es muy trabajador_, Mi amigo es muy simpátic_.**

9   Translate these phrases into Spanish: *in the north-east, near York, between the beach and the town, on the seafront*

10 Which is the odd one out among these adjectives, and why? **abierto, alegre, antipático, cariñoso, amable, generoso**

11 If you hear someone described as **No tiene pelos en la lengua**, what sort of person would you expect them to be?

12 Rearrange **se su en encuentra Valencia casa dónde ¿?** to ask about a friend's house.

13 Which of these means *polluted*: **cómodo, concurrido, contaminado, congestionado**?

14 What do you need to add to **Tengo alergia al ...** to say *I've got a wheat allergy*?

15 Sort these adjectives into pairs with opposite meanings: **ancho, montañoso, limpio, ruidoso, nuevo, llano, sucio, estrecho, tranquilo, viejo**

tres
what you do

What do you do? is one of the first questions that tends to be asked when people are getting to know each other. The Spanish verb **hacer** means *to do* but, when work is concerned, the key verb is **trabajar**, so you ask what someone does for a living with **¿En qué trabaja?**

It's tempting to think that you only need the language to say what you do, plus some questions. But when you ask the questions, you might be confronted with a wide variety of replies, so don't be too selective in the vocabulary you learn. If you're neither a pilot nor a postman, you're never going to want to say **Soy piloto** or **Soy cartero/a** … but somebody might well say it to you.

Business hierarchy is more in evidence in Spain than in English-speaking countries. Professional titles are more prevalent; introductions are likely to consist of a surname or a full name, together with the role in the company.

Even if the culture in the places you visit seems to you to be casual, it's as well not to assume that immediate informality will break the ice quickly and forge strong relationships: uninvited use of **tú** and first names may instead take some people out of their comfort zone.

saying what you do

Typical conversations about what you do start with questions like:
¿En qué trabaja(s)? ¿Qué hace(s)? ¿A qué te dedicas?/¿A qué se dedica?
What do you do for a living?
¿Trabaja usted?/¿Trabajas? *Are you working? Do you work?*
¿Cuál es tu/su profesión? *What work do you do?*

The answer often begins with **soy**, followed straightaway by the job, without *a/an*: **Soy entrenador personal.** *I'm a personal trainer.*
Soy diseñadora/estudiante. *I'm a designer/a student.*

wordbank

agente de bolsa *stockbroker*
agente de policía *police officer*
agente de viajes *travel agent*
agente inmobiliario *estate agent*
albañil *construction worker*
asesor(a) *consultant, advisor*
azafato/a *flight attendant*
banquero/a *banker*
bombero/a *fire fighter*
camionero/a *lorry driver*
canguro *nanny*
cantante *singer*
cartero/a *postman/woman*
chófer *driver*
científico/a *scientist*
cocinero/a /chef *cook/chef*
controlador(a) aéreo/a *air traffic controller*
coreógrafo/a *choreographer*

diseñador(a) de páginas web *web designer*
docente *teacher, lecturer*
enfermero/a *nurse*
fontanero/a *plumber*
funcionario/a *civil servant*
futbolista *footballer*
guardia de seguridad *security guard*
historiador(a) *historian*
informático/a *computer scientist*
investigador(a) *researcher*
modelo *model*
niñero/a *childminder*
oficinista *office worker*
periodista *journalist*
piloto *pilot*
político/a *politician*
socorrista *lifeguard*

Instead of **soy**, you can use **Trabajo como ...** *I work as a ...*:
Trabajo como bombero *I'm a fireman*. However, many people prefer to say what area they work in: **Trabajo en relaciones públicas** *I work in public relations*.

jobs you can guess

Many Spanish occupations end in **-ista**. They're often the equivalent of English words ending in -ist: **analista** *analyst*, **dentista** *dentist*, **economista** *economist*, **florista** *florist*. However, some **-ista** words have a different ending in English: **electricista** *electrician*, **esteticista** *beautician*, **taxista** *taxi driver*.

The **-ista** words have the same ending for males and females: *a dentist* can be **un dentista** or **una dentista**.

An English *-ologist* generally ends in **-ólogo** in Spanish: **biólogo, ecólogo, ornitólogo, geólogo, ginecólogo, psicólogo, enólogo**. These days, the tendency is to change the **-o** to **-a** for women.

not the 9 to 5

Soy (trabajador) autónomo. *I'm freelance/self-employed.*
Soy/Estoy jubilado/a. *I'm retired.*
Soy ama/amo de casa. *I'm a stay-at-home mother/father.*
Soy madre trabajadora. *I'm a working mother.*
Estoy en paro. *I'm unemployed.*
Estoy desempleado/a. *I'm unemployed.*
Busco trabajo. *I'm job hunting.* lit. *I'm looking for a job.*

Trabajo ... *I work ...*
> **... desde casa.** *... from home.*
> **... a tiempo parcial.** *... part time.*
> **... a tiempo completo.** *... full time.*

No trabajo. *I don't work.*
Cuido de mi madre/mis hijos. *I look after my mother/children.*
Hago trabajo voluntario. *I volunteer/do charity work.*
Tengo mi propio negocio. *I have my own business.*

With a few simple changes, you can adapt what you've learnt to talk about other people. To say what someone else does, you replace soy with es and trabajo with trabaja: Mi padre es cantante, Mi compañera es fontanera, Mi hermano trabaja como farmacéutico. Try it out by choosing a couple of the people you described in Chapter 2 and adding what they do to your description.

discussing work

¿Dónde trabajas/trabaja? *Where do you work?*
The answer might be in a country or a city or a specific workplace, in which case you begin with **Trabajo en ...** *I work in/at ...* More generally, you can say **Trabajo en el sector ...** *I work in the ... sector/field*. You use **Trabajo para ...** to say who you work for.

Trabajo en ...
> ... **Londres/Madrid/París.** ... *London/Madrid/Paris.*
> ... **una agencia de apuestas.** ... *a betting shop.*
> ... **un centro de llamadas.** ... *a call centre.*
> ... **una consulta médica.** ... *a doctor's surgery.*
> ... **una escuela.** ... *a school.*
> ... **una fábrica.** ... *a factory.*
> ... **un taller de coches.** ... *a garage.*

Trabajo en el sector ...
> ... **turístico.** ... *in tourism.*
> ... **agrícola.** ... *in agriculture.*
> ... **minorista.** ... *in retail.*
> ... **público.** ... *in the public sector.*
> ... **sanitario.** ... *in the health sector.*

Trabajo en relaciones públicas. *I work in public relations.*

¿Para quién trabajas/trabaja? *Who do you work for?*
Trabajo para ... *I work for ...*
> ... **un banco internacional.** ... *an international bank.*
> ... **una bodega.** ... *a winery.*
> ... **una organización benéfica.** ... *a charity.*
> ... **un contable.** ... *an accountant.*
> ... **una empresa de software.** ... *a software company.*
> ... **el Ministerio de Medio Ambiente.** ... *the Department for the Environment.*
> ... **una empresa multinacional de telecomunicaciones.** ... *a multinational telecommunications corporation.*

To say what you used to do, you simply replace **soy** with era, and both **trabajo** and **trabaja** with trabajaba: Era **profesora** *I was a teacher*, Trabajaba **desde casa** *I used to work from home*, Trabajaba **como chófer** *I used to work as a driver*.

¿Cuál es tu/su puesto de trabajo? *What's your role?*
Soy responsable de **control de calidad.** *I'm in charge of Quality Control.*
Soy gerente de **recursos humanos.** *I'm a human resources manager.*
Soy coordinador(a) de **proyectos.** *I'm a project co-ordinator.*
Trabajo en **la oficina de prensa.** *I work in the press office.*
Yo también **trabajo en la oficina de prensa**. *I work in the press office too.*
Informo **directamente al jefe.** *I report directly to the boss.*
Soy **director(a) adjunto/a.** *I'm deputy director/assistant manager.*
Soy **técnico de mantenimiento.** *I'm the maintenance man.*
Soy **el burro de carga.** *I'm just the dogsbody.*

¿Cuál es tu/su especialidad? *What's your field of expertise?*
Gestiono **el sistema informático.** *I manage the IT system.*
Hago **investigación.** *I do research.*
Me ocupo de **la salud y seguridad.** *I deal with Health and Safety.*
Me ocupo de **la página web de la empresa.** *I look after the company website.*
Me ocupo de **las tareas administrativas.** *I do the admin.*
Dirijo **el departamento.** *I run the department.*
Me encargo del **almacén.** *I'm in charge of the warehouse.*

working words

Currar is a colloquial and very widespread way of saying **trabajar.**
Ahora voy a acostarme porque mañana tengo que currar. *I'm going to bed now because I've got to work tomorrow.*

Currante *hard-working* means the same as **trabajador(a).**
¡Qué currante eres! What a hard worker you are.

Un enchufe is a *connection,* someone who will be able to get you work: **Estar enchufado/a** *to be well connected.*
Pedro está enchufado; está aquí por su tío. *Pedro's well connected; he's here because of his uncle.*
No tiene este puesto por sus habilidades sino por sus enchufes. *He hasn't got this job because of his abilities but rather through his connections.*

how regular verbs work

A conversation about work or any other topic needs a knowledge of how verbs function. In English it's often a simple matter of adding -s for *he/she/it* (*I work, we work, he or she works*) but in Spanish the ending of the verb changes for each subject.

Trabajo *I work* comes from **trabajar** *(to) work*. **Trabajar** is the infinitive, which is the form used in a dictionary, and every Spanish infinitive has the ending **-ar**, **-er** or **-ir**.

Removing that ending leaves you with a stem to which you add other endings, according to who is the subject of the verb. This actually makes the words **yo, tú, usted** etc. redundant most of the time.

Present-tense endings differ only slightly for each group of verbs; the majority of the endings in the **-ir** group are the same as those of the **-er** group.

infinitive (*to*)	-ar	-er	-ir
yo *I*	-o	-o	-o
tú *you*	-as	-es	-es
usted *you*	-a	-e	-e
él/ella *he/she/it*	-a	-e	-e
nosotros/as *we*	-amos	-emos	-imos
vosotros/as *you*	-áis	-éis	-ís
ustedes *you*	-an	-en	-en
ellos/ellas *they*	-an	-en	-en

Once you're familiar with these endings, you can use the present tense of any regular verb, and it takes surprisingly little time for the association of **-o** with *I*, **-amos** with *we*, etc, to become hard-wired in the brain.

ayudar *to help*	**ayud**o *I help*	**ayud**amos *we help*
llegar *to arrive*	**lleg**o *I arrive*	**lleg**amos *we arrive*
esperar *to wait*	**esper**o *I wait*	**esper**amos *we wait*
preguntar *to ask*	**pregunt**as *you ask*	**pregunt**áis *you ask*
vender *to sell*	**vend**es *you sell*	**vend**éis *you sell*
leer *to read*	**le**es *you read*	**le**éis *you read*
depender *to depend*	**depend**e *it depends*	**depend**en *they depend*
abrir *to open*	**abr**e *he/she, it opens*	**abr**en *they open*
escribir *to write*	**escrib**es *you write*	**escrib**ís *you write*
vivir *to live*	**viv**o *I live*	**viv**imos *we live*

reflexive verbs

The infinitives of some verbs have -se tacked on to them so that in a dictionary they end in **-arse**, **-erse** or **-irse** These are reflexive verbs, and the English translation often includes or implies *self*.

> **aburrir**se *to get bored*
> **acordar**se **de** *to remember*
> **acostar**se *to go to bed*
> **casar**se *to get married*
> **divertir**se *to enjoy* *oneself*
> **levantar**se *to get (oneself) up*
> **llamar**se *to be called,* lit. *to call* *oneself*
> **ocupar**se **de** *to look after* lit. *to occupy* *oneself with*
> **preguntar**se *to wonder* lit. *to ask* *oneself*
> **preocupar**se *to worry (oneself)*
> **sentar**se *to sit (oneself) down*
> **vestir**se *to get (oneself) dressed*

Se means *oneself*, and is replaced by **me, te, se, nos, os** or **se** to say *myself, yourself, ourselves*, etc: **debo sentarme** *I need to sit (myself) down*.

When not in the infinitive, a reflexive verb loses **se** and behaves like any other verb, but with the addition of a separate **me, te, se, nos, os** or **se** beforehand:

	levantarse	*to get (oneself) up*	
yo	me	**levanto**	*I get up*
tú	te	**levantas**	*you get up*
usted	se	**levanta**	*you get up*
él/ella	se	**levanta**	*he/she/it gets up*
nosotros/as	nos	**levantamos**	*we get up*
vosotros/as	os	**levantáis**	*you get up*
ustedes	se	**levantan**	*you get up*
ellos/ellas	se	**levantan**	*they get up*

Me llamo Claudia. *My name's Claudia.* lit. *I call* myself *Claudia.*
Se casan en mayo. *They're getting married in May.*
No nos preocupamos. *We're not worrying.*

how long have you been ...?

There are a few ways of asking how long you've been doing something:
¿Desde cuándo trabajas aquí?
¿Cuánto tiempo hace que trabajas aquí?
Both mean: *How long have you been working here?*

In Spanish, you don't say you have been doing something for/since ..., you say
I am doing something for/since ..., using the present tense. *For* is **desde hace**
and *since* is **desde**.

Trabajo **como supervisor/gerente general** desde hace ... *I've been a
supervisor/general manager for ...*
    ... (unos) seis meses. ... *(about) six months.*
    ... un año y medio/diez años. ... *a year and a half/ten years.*
    ... ¡ufff! un montón de años. ... *years and years.*

Trabajo **aquí** desde ... *I've been working here since ...*
    ... el año pasado. ... *last year.*
    ... septiembre. ... *September.*
    ... dos mil trece. ... *2013.*

Llevar

Llevar is often used to express how long something has been
going on:
¿Cuánto tiempo llevas trabajando aquí? *How long have you been
working here?*
Llevo dos años en España. *I've been in Spain for two years.*

The verb **llevar** has several other different meanings, one of which
is *to carry*:
Déjame llevarlo. *Let me carry it.*

It can also mean *to wear*:
Voy a llevar mi traje nuevo. *I am going to wear my new suit.*

hacer *to do, to make*

Hacer is a widely used verb, meaning *to do* or *to make*, but it's also used in ways that don't feature *do* or *make* in English. It has an unexpected first person **yo hago**, but is otherwise regular: **tú haces**, **él/ella/usted hace**, etc.

Hago ejercicio todos los días. *I do some exercise every day.*
Lo hago ahora mismo. *I'll do it straightaway.*
¿Qué haces? *What are you doing? What are you making?*
¿Qué trabajo hace? *What work do you do?*

It's used with some weather expressions (page 102):
¿Qué tiempo hace? *What's the weather like?*
Hace buen tiempo/mal tiempo. *The weather's lovely/awful.*
Hace frío/calor/sol/viento. *It's cold/hot/sunny/windy.*

... and in many common phrases:
hacer una visita *to pay a visit*
hacer cola *to queue*
hacer una pregunta *to ask a question*
hacer las maletas *to pack*

Hacer falta means *to be necessary/to need*:
Hacen falta cincuenta euros. *We need fifty euros.*
¿Hace falta algo? *Do we need anything?*
No hace falta reservar. *It's not necessary to book.*

Hace also means *ago*:
hace tres días *three days ago*
hace poco *a short while ago*

---

handiwork

Hacer una chapuza is *to bodge something*:
Aquel fontanero siempre hace chapuzas. *That plumber always bodges things.*

Someone who's good with their hands is known as **un(a) manitas**, literally *little hands*, deriving from **la mano** *hand*. The opposite of **un(a) manitas** is **un(a) manazas**, someone who is very clumsy:
Mi tío es un manitas, pero mi padre, en cambio, es un manazas. *My uncle is good with his hands but my father, by contrast, is very clumsy.*

talking the talk

Javier	(*On phone*) ¿Y qué tal el trabajo ...?
	Venga. Adiós Caro. Que te vaya bien.
Isabel	¿Quién es Caro? ¿Tu novia?
Javier	No. Es mi hermana mayor. Se llama Carolina. Tiene un problema en el trabajo.
Isabel	¿En qué trabaja?
Javier	Es enóloga. Trabaja en una bodega, una empresa pequeña. Es responsable de todo el proceso de la producción del vino, desde la uva hasta la botella que compras en un supermercado. Informa directamente al jefe ... ¡mi padre!
Isabel	¿Tu padre es el jefe? Una empresa familiar. ¿Y tu madre trabaja en la bodega también?
Javier	Trabaja en la oficina ... a tiempo parcial porque ayuda a sus padres. Su padre, mi abuelo, tiene setenta y dos años y es diabético. No está bien.
Isabel	¿Viven todos en Medina de Rioseco?
Javier	Sí.
Isabel	Pero tú no.
Javier	¿Tu madre trabaja?
Isabel	Sí, trabaja en una consulta médica, en las afueras.
Javier	¿Y qué hace exactamente?
Isabel	Es enfermera. Mi hermana también es enfermera.
Javier	¿En qué trabaja tu amiga, Sophie?
Isabel	Trabaja en relaciones públicas ... desde hace unos seis meses. Es autónoma, trabaja desde casa.

verb practice 2

1. Write the correct present-tense forms of these verbs.

   a. **esperar** *to wait* — tú ....
   b. **cambiar** *to change* — ustedes ....
   c. **comprar** *to buy* — vosotros/as ....
   d. **durar** *to last* — .... (it)
   e. **poner** *to put* — nosotros/as ....
   f. **vender** *to sell* — usted ....
   g. **comer** *to eat* — yo ....
   h. **vivir** *to live* — ella ....
   i. **escribir** *to write* — nosotros/as ....
   j. **abrir** *to open* — yo ....

2. The verb **hacer** is widely used. Fill in the gaps in these sentences with its correct form in the present tense and then give the meaning.

   a. Yo .... ejercicio todos los días.
   b. ¿Qué .... tú?
   c. ¿Qué trabajo .... ella?
   d. .... buen tiempo.
   e. Nosotros .... cola para comprar las entradas.
   f. Mis tíos nos .... una visita todos los meses.
   g. ¿Cuánto tiempo .... que vivís aquí?

3. Decide whether **me, te, se, nos** or **os** belongs in the gap:

   a. ¿Cómo ... llama el perro? *What's the dog called?*
   b. ... ocupan del almacén. *They look after the warehouse.*
   c. No ... levantamos muy temprano. *We don't get up very early.*
   d. Lola ... aburre fácilmente. *Lola gets bored easily.*
   e. ¿ ... acuerdas? *Do you remember?*
   f. Mi hermana ... casa en abril. *My sister's getting married in April.*
   g. ¿ ... divertís todos? *Are you all having a good time?*

1   Match the people with their workplace:
    microbiólogo, mecánico, docente, cocinera, enfermero, canguro
    universidad, laboratorio, hospital, taller de coches, restaurante
    What does the person left over do?

2   How would you say in English: **Soy médico, Somos dentistas, Es**
    funcionaria?

3   What two words do you add to **Trabajo aquí .... quince**
    años to say you've been working here for 15 years?

4   What do you think the Spanish is for *archaeologist* and
    meteorologist? And what do you think these jobs are: **reumatólogo,**
    sociólogo and **egiptólogo**?

5   If you needed a plumber, would you ask for a **fontanero, bombero,**
    cocinero or **camionero**?

6   What two words mean *hard-working*?

7   How would you say that you work a) from home b) part time c) full
    time?

8   How might you tell someone in Spanish that your partner is self-
    employed?

9   What's another way of saying **Estoy en paro**?

10 Where do people employed **en el sector minorista, en el sector**
    público, en el sector sanitario, en una fábrica work?

11 How would you ask someone what their role is?

12 Decide from the verbs whether these questions relate to **tú, usted**
    or **vosotros/as**: ¿Te encargas de la página web? ¿A qué hora os
    acostáis? ¿Se ocupa de la seguridad? ¿No se aburre nunca?

13 Put the correct word in the gap. Choose from **dirijo, gestiono** and
    hago. a) .... **el sistema informático.** *I manage the IT system.*
    b) .... **investigación.** *I do research.* c) .... **el departamento.** *I run*
    the department.

14 Rearrange these words to form a sentence, then say what it means
    in English: **de la la me página ocupo de web empresa**

15 Change these sentences from the present to the past. **Trabajo como**
    analista, Soy cocinero, Juan trabaja en una consulta médica.

cuatro
the art of conversation

Once you're past the stage of exchanging basic information with someone, you tend to move on to more general conversation. A conversation in your native language flows without awkward pauses or prolonged silences; it feels comfortable and includes comments and prompts, questions and exclamations.

As a learner, you may not always be able to say as much as you'd like, but you can still contribute simply by knowing how to keep a conversation going. There are a number of strategies you can use to show that you're properly engaged in a conversation. Gestures, eye contact, a smile, positive body language or a nod at the right time all show that you're actively listening and following what's being said — but they're not nearly as satisfying as being able to offer an exclamation or an appropriate comment.

A lot of the words that are needed for this are very short and easy to remember: **sí, ya, claro,** for instance, are all used to show that you agree with what someone is saying. There are plenty of simple phrases you can use too, such as: **¡No me digas!** *Tell me about it! You don't say!* or **¡Estás de broma!** *You must be joking!*

following what's being said

At times, Spanish is spoken very rapidly. Nobody will mind if you ask for help now and again or find it necessary to slow the conversation down so you can understand.

Perdón/Perdone ... *Excuse me* ...
Disculpa, pero ... *I beg your pardon, but* ... **(tú)**
Disculpe, pero ... *I beg your pardon, but* ... **(usted)**
Disculpe por la interrupción, pero ... *Sorry for interrupting, but* ...

No entiendo. *I don't understand.*
No he entendido. *I haven't understood.*
No sé si he entendido bien. *I don't know if I've understood properly.*

¿Qué quiere decir ...? *What does ... mean?*
¿Qué significa ...? *What does ... mean?*
... significa ..., ¿verdad? .... *means ..., doesn't it?*
¿Qué quiere decir/significa azafata? *What does **azafata** mean?*
Azafata quiere decir *flight attendant*, ¿verdad? *Azafata means flight attendant, doesn't it?*
¿Qué has/ha dicho? *What did you say?*
¿Me lo puedes/puede repetir, por favor? *Can you repeat that, please?*
¿Puedes hablar más despacio? *Can you speak more slowly?*
¿Te importaría explicarlo? *Would you mind explaining it?*
¿Te importaría repetir eso? *Would you mind repeating that?*
¿Le importaría explicarlo/repetirlo? *Would you mind explaining/repeating that?*

You can show that you're following by echoing what's been said before and offering a relevant comment or question.

-**Mi cuñado trabaja en China.** *My brother-in-law works in China.*
-**¿En China? ¿Ah sí? ¿Dónde en China?** *In China? Really? Whereabouts in China?*

- **Un amigo mío trabaja para RTVE.** *A friend of mine works for RTVE.*
- **¿RTVE?** *RTVE?*
- **La televisión española. Es presentador de programas de noticias.** *Spanish TV. He's a news presenter.*
- **Ah, sí. ¿Cómo se llama?** *Right, what's his name?*

making yourself understood

Sometimes you need to know if you're getting your message across.

¿Me entiendes/entiende/me entendéis? *Do you understand me?*
¿Me explico? *Am I making sense?*
No sé si me explico bien. *I don't know if I'm explaining things very well.*

If you're stuck for a word, say so:

He olvidado la palabra. *I've forgotten the word.*
No encuentro la palabra correcta. *I can't find the right word.*
Me falta la palabra. *The word escapes me.*
Lo tengo en la punta de la lengua. *It's on the tip of my tongue.*
¿Cómo se llama esto en español? *What's this called in Spanish?*
¿Cómo se dice ... en español? *What's the Spanish for ...?*
Se me ha ido el santo al cielo. *I've totally forgotten.* lit. *The saint's left me and gone to heaven!*

¿Cómo se llama esto? *What's this called?* is useful if the word you're searching for is something that's within sight.

- **¿Cómo se llama esto?** (pointing at microwave)
- **Este aparato se llama microondas.**

If not, paraphrasing can be effective.

No sé cómo se llama. *I don't know what it's called.*
Es lo contrario de ... *It's the opposite of ...*
Es un tipo de ... *It's a sort of ...*
Es un poco como ... *It's a bit like ...*
Se parece a ... *He/She/It looks like ...*
Sirve para medir/calcular ... *It's used to measure/calculate ...*

You can always resort to words like **la cosa, el chisme** *thingy, thingamajig* or, if all else fails, gestures and mime:
Era así de grande. *It was this big.*
Tenía la cara así. *His face was like this.*

educated guesswork

Many Spanish words are instantly recognisable to an English speaker, e.g. **adulto, animal, dólar, elefante, error, familia, música, momento, elegante, interesante, medicina, moderno, universal**. These are called cognates, meaning *born together*, because they share a common ancestor.

Knowing which English words have a Spanish cognate is not as straightforward, but there are pointers that raise the odds of an educated guess turning out to be correct.

Noun endings can provide clues, e.g.

🇬🇧	🇪🇸	
-tion	**-ción**	**atención, conversación, nación**
-ism	**-ismo**	**anglicismo, idealismo, turismo**
-ist	**-ista**	**ciclista, dentista, hedonista**
-nt	**-nte**	**infante, paciente, accidente**
-phy	**-fía**	**geografía, filosofía, fotografía**
-ty	**-dad**	**humanidad, universidad, ciudad, realidad**

... as can the endings of adjectives, e.g.

-ary	**-ario**	**intermediario, ordinario, subsidiario**
-ic	**-ico**	**fantástico, lógico, mágico**
-ive	**-ivo**	**agresivo, excesivo, persuasivo**
-ous	**-oso**	**fabuloso, escandaloso, glamuroso**

... and adverbs:

-ly	**-mente**	**perfectamente, curiosamente, efectivamente**

amigos falsos *false friends*

Not all words mean what they appear to mean, however, e.g.

asistir a *to attend*	*to assist* **ayudar**
actualmente *at the present time*	*actually* **en realidad**
estar embarazada *to be pregnant*	*to be embarrassed* **tener vergüenza**
estar constipado/a *to have a cold*	*to be constipated* **estar estreñido/a**
el éxito *success*	*exit* **la salida**
la librería *bookshop*	*library* **la biblioteca**
el nudo *knot*	*nude* **desnudo/a**
los preservativos *condoms*	*preservatives* **los conservantes**
el rape *monkfish*	*rape* **la violación**
simpático/a *nice*	*sympathetic* **compasivo/a**

showing empathy

A well-chosen interjection shows that you're listening and understanding the mood of the conversation.

¡Muy bien! *Great! Well said!*
¡Genial! ¡Fantástico! *Well said! Bravo!*
¡Cierto! *True!* **¡Correcto!** *That's right!*
¡Exacto! ¡Exactamente! ¡Precisamente! *Exactly! Spot on!*
¡Claro! *Of course!*
¡Eso es! *That's right!*

Like English, Spanish has expressions that can equally well convey interest, admiration, incredulity, indignation, amusement, amazement, concern, fascination or horror, depending on your tone of voice and expression.

¿De veras? ¿De verdad? *Really?* **¿En serio?** *Seriously?*
¡Madre mía! ¡Ay Dios mío! *Wow! Goodness me!*
¡Vaya! *Damn! Oh no! Wow!* **¡Vaya pobre!** *Poor thing!*
¡Qué va! *No way! Not at all!*
¡No me digas/diga! *You don't say! Oh, come on!*
¡Por amor de Dios! *Good grief!*
¡Dios mío! *OMG!*
¡Fíjate!/¡Fíjese! *Fancy that! Well I never!*
¡Ojalá! *If only! I wish!*
¡Caramba! *Wow! Good grief! Damn!*
¡Estás de broma! *You're joking!*
¡Qué suerte tienes/tiene! *Lucky you!*
¡Cuéntame! *Tell me!*
¡Venga ya! ¡Anda ya! *Impossible! No way!*
¡Qué bueno! *How funny/amusing!*
¡Que me parto! *I'm laughing out loud!*
¡Me alegro mucho! *I'm really happy for you!*

You might also hear **¡Hostia!** and **¡Hostias!** – but be wary of using them as they're considered unacceptable by many because they refer to the host in the Catholic communion. They're often replaced by **¡Ostras!** *oysters,* which *is* acceptable: **!Ostras! ¡Qué suerte!** *Wow! What a stroke of luck!*
Other inoffensive substitutes for a profanity or a vulgarity include **¡miércoles!** *Wednesday!* and **¡jolín!** or **¡jolines!**, which have no actual meaning:
¡Jolines! No tengo la llave. *Damn it, I haven't got the key!*

commenting

When you want your response to be specific, you can use **¡Qué** followed by a noun, meaning *What a ...!* or sometimes *How ...!*
¡Qué alegría! *What a joy!*
¡Qué alivio! *What a relief!*
¡Qué asco! *How disgusting!*
¡Qué barbaridad! *How awful! How amazing!*
¡Qué buena idea! *What a good idea!*
¡Qué casualidad! *What a coincidence!*
¡Qué desilusión! *How disappointing!*
¡Qué ganas! *How appealing!*
¡Qué lástima! *What a pity!*
¡Qué lata! *What a nuisance!*
¡Qué lío! *What a mess!*
¡Qué logro! *What an achievement! What a success!*
¡Qué miedo! *How scary!*
¡Qué molestia! *How annoying!*
¡Qué rollo! *What a drag!*
¡Qué aburrimiento! *How boring!*
¡Qué sorpresa! *What a surprise!*
¡Qué tontería! *How silly!*

It's also useful to have a ready supply of adjectives. They work on their own or they too can be used with **qué** to mean *how* or *what*:
¡Impecable! *Impeccable!* **¡Imposible!** *Impossible!*
¡Qué interesante! *How interesting!* **¡Qué bonito!** *What a sight! What a performance! How beautiful!* **¡Qué rico!** *How delicious!*

Don't forget words like **muy, demasiado, tan, bastante, algo:**
¡Muy emocionante! *Very exciting!*
¡Demasiado tarde! *Too late!*
Algo desagradable. *Rather unpleasant.*
Muy simpático. *Really nice.*
Algo triste. *A bit sad.*

Simple prompts are very effective at moving a conversation along:
¿Y entonces? *And then?* **¿Y después?** *And afterwards?*
¡Cuéntame más! *Tell me more!*
Continúa, por favor. *Please continue.*
¡No me dejes en vilo! *Don't leave me in suspense.*
Y, ¿qué más? *And what else?*

wordbank

admiration, appreciation
afortunado *lucky*
agradable *pleasant*
amable *kind*
amistoso *friendly*
educado *polite*
encantador *delightful, charming*
espléndido *amazing*
estupendo *superb, great*
excelente *excellent*
exquisito *exquisite*
fantástico *fantastic*
fascinante *fascinating*
generoso *generous*
hermoso *beautiful*
honesto *honest*
impresionante *impressive*
inteligente *intelligent*
interesante *interesting, exciting*
listo *clever*
maravilloso *wonderful*
simpático *nice, kind*
sincero *sincere, honest*
valiente *brave*

concern, empathy
antipático *unpleasant*
decepcionante *disappointing*
desafortunado *unfortunate*
desagradable *nasty, unpleasant*
grave *serious*
horrible *horrible*
imprevisto *unexpected*
inconveniente *inconvenient*
pesado *tedious*
triste *sad*

horror, sympathy
asqueroso *gross, disgusting*
estresante *stressful*
desastroso *disastrous*
horrendo *horrendous*
odioso *hateful*
terrible *terrible*
trágico *tragic*

astonishment, amusement
absurdo *ridiculous*
curioso *odd*
divertido *amusing*
extraño *strange, weird*
extraordinario *amazing, extraordinary*
gracioso *funny*
increíble *incredible*
loco *crazy, mad*
raro *unusual*
tonto *daft*

general
cómodo *convenient*
conveniente *advisable*
difícil *difficult*
eficaz *effective*
especial *special*
grande *big*
interesante *interesting*
original *original*
pequeño *small*
práctico *handy, practical*
razonable *reasonable, realistic*
sencillo *simple*
serio *serious, reliable*
útil *useful*

 Find six of these words that you wouldn't have been able to guess. Write them down and think of sentences where you might use them. Then, say them out loud. For instance: Hoy es lunes y hace mal tiempo. **Today is Monday and the weather's bad.** ¡Qué pesado!

adding structure and fluency

Conversations tend to include words like *well, besides, anyway, let's see, frankly, however, in fact*. Some of them add structure to what you say, others add emphasis, while some simply bring a natural feel to a conversation. They also give you time to think. For instance, you'll hear people starting a conversation with **Lo que pasa es que ...** *The thing is ...* as they prepare for what they're really going to say. Other words which help provide fluency are:

bueno, entonces, pues *well then; so; mmm, let's see*
y *and*, **también** *also*, **además** *what's more, furthermore*
pero *but*, **sin embargo** *however*, **en cambio** *instead*
aún, todavía *still, (and) yet*
por lo tanto, por eso *so, therefore*
de todos modos, en cualquier caso *anyway*
claramente *clearly*, **obviamente** *obviously*
de hecho, en realidad *in fact, indeed*
Total, que ... *So, it turns out that ...*
sabes (tú)/sabe (usted), ya sabe(s) *you know*
a decir verdad *to be honest*, **francamente** *frankly*
en breve *to cut a long story short*
por ejemplo *for example*
es decir *that is, in other words, the thing is*
a ver *let's see*

Francamente, es una idea fantástica. *Frankly, it's a great idea!*
Total, que al final no vamos a la playa. *So, it turns out that in the end we are not going to the beach.*
Todavía no entiendo. *I still don't understand.*
Por eso estamos aquí. *That is why we are here.*

ya – a small but very useful word

Ya, which punctuates many Spanish conversations, is used in several ways. In phrases like **¡Basta ya!** or **¡Ya basta!** *That's enough!* and **¡Corta ya!** *Shut up!* it doesn't have an actual translation but adds emphasis. It's used in a similar way in expressions involving time: **Ya era hora** *It was about time*, **Ya me contarás** *You'll tell me later*. It can mean *already*: **Ya lo he hecho** *I've already done it*. And it's also a very handy conversation filler: **Ya veo** *I see.*

food and wine small talk

Sitting round the dinner table with family and friends is central to Spanish life, and conversation is as much part of the experience as the food and drink. **La sobremesa** is the word for this period of post-meal relaxation.

¿Tienes hambre/sed? *Are you hungry/thirsty?*
Tengo mucha hambre, ¿a qué hora comemos? *I'm starving: what time are we eating?*
Me muero de sed. *I'm dying of thirst.*
Se me hace la boca agua. *It's making my mouth water.*
Mi hija come como un pajarito. *My daughter eats like a little bird.*
¡Que aproveche! *Enjoy your meal.*

I'm so hungry I could eat a horse has various animal equivalents in Spanish: **Tengo tanta hambre que me comería una vaca** *a cow*, **un elefante** *an elephant*, as well as **un caballo** *a horse*. In Latin America, you might hear: **Tengo tanta hambre que me comería un burro entero** *a whole donkey*.

¿Está bueno/a? *Is it good?*
¡Qué sabroso/a! *How tasty!*
¡Qué delicioso/a! ¡Qué rico/a! *So delicious!*
El venado, ¡qué bien huele! *How good the venison smells!*
Las almejas, ¡qué bien huelen! *How good the clams smell!*
¡Qué bien sabe/saben! *How good it tastes/they taste!*
¡Está/Están para chuparse los dedos! *It/They are fingerlickin' good!*
El guiso está buenísimo/a. *The casserole is superb.*
Es un poco fuerte/dulce/picante. *It's a bit strong/sweet/spicy.*
Estoy lleno/a y no puedo más. *I'm full and can't eat another thing.*

La cuenta, por favor. *The bill please.*
Invito yo. *My treat.*
Invitamos nosotros. *Our treat.*
Esta ronda la pago yo. *I'm paying for this round.*
Paguemos a escote. *Let's go Dutch.*
Paguemos a medias. *Let's share the cost.*

Not all food expressions should be taken too literally. **Ser un chorizo/una choriza** means *to be a thief* and **estar como un fideo** *to be as thin as a rake* (lit. *a noodle*), while **estar de mala leche** (lit. *bad milk*) means *to be in a bad mood* and **estar como una sopa** *soaked to the skin*. **Es pan comido** is the equivalent of *a piece of cake*.

¿Quieres una copa de vino blanco? *Would you like a glass of white wine?*
¿Quiere probar este tinto? *Do you want to try this red (wine)?*
¡Qué intenso! *How intense!*
¡Qué suave! *How smooth!*
Este es un vino con mucho cuerpo. *This one is a full-bodied wine.*
Es algo afrutado, ¿verdad? *It's quite fruity, isn't it?*
¿Es muy seco? *Is it very dry?*
¡Salud! *Cheers!*

Solo una gota/un vasito para mí ... *Just a drop/a small glass for me ...*
     ... ya que tomo medicación para ... *... because I take medication for ...*
     ... la hipertensión/la diabetes. *... high blood pressure/diabetes.*
Estoy embarazada (de cinco meses). *I'm (five months) pregnant.*

The Spanish are always delighted to answer questions about their wines.
¿Qué significa **crianza?** *What does* ***crianza*** *mean?*
Un vino de crianza pasa un año – como mínimo – en una barrica de roble. *A* ***crianza*** *wine spends a year – at the very least – in an oak barrel.*

¿Qué es **un tinto de verano?** *What's a* ***tinto de verano?***
Es vino tinto con gaseosa. *It's red wine with sparkling lemonade.*

¿Qué quiere decir **calimocho?** *What does* ***calimocho*** *mean?*
Un calimocho es una mezcla de vino tinto y Coca-Cola. *A* ***calimocho*** *is a mixture of red wine and cola.*

Spain's extraordinary range of wines includes **vino tinto** and **vino blanco**, as well as **cava** *sparkling wine* and **jerez** *sherry*. Rosé comes in two forms, the pale pink **clarete** and the much rosier-coloured **rosado**.
La etiqueta *wine label* will tell you the **bodega** *winery*, **cosecha** *vintage*, **cepa** *grape variety* and **añejo** *how long it's been aged*. There's a big gap between a **vino joven** *young wine* and a **gran reserva** a five-year-old wine, of which at least two have been spent ageing in oak barrels.
Top quality wines boast the initials **D.O. (denominación de origen)**. Cheaper wines are labelled **vino de mesa** *table wine, house wine*. These or **vino joven** are the wines used for **tinto de verano** and **calimocho**.

talking the talk

Rodrigo	¡Fíjate! ¡Qué suerte! El plato del día es lacón con grelos.
Isabel	Disculpa, pero no entiendo, ¿puedes repetir, por favor?
Rodrigo	Bueno, lacón con grelos es una especialidad de mi región. El lacón es un poco como el jamón, ¿sabes? Los grelos son un tipo de verduras. Tienen un sabor muy rico. ¿Quieres probar este plato?
Isabel	Sí, ¿cómo no? Ya se me hace la boca agua.

Isabel	¡Qué rico está! La salsa está muy buena y el lacón está para chuparse los dedos.
Rodrigo	¡Qué bien! ¿Quieres tomar postre?
Isabel	Bueno ... gracias, pero no puedo más.
Rodrigo	Te entiendo; es un plato riquísimo, pero llena mucho. ¿Quieres tomar un café y un chupito?
Isabel	Solo café para mí ...

Isabel	Dime, ¿por qué estas aquí? ¿Por trabajo?
Rodrigo	Sí. Actualmente soy responsable de control de calidad.
Isabel	¿De verdad? ¡Qué interesante! ¿Desde cuándo trabajas en eso?
Rodrigo	¡Un mes! ... ¿Una copa de cava?
Isabel	Pues ... una copita. ¡Salud! ¡Enhorabuena! Me alegro mucho.

las verduras = *vegetables*
un chupito = *a shot* (of liquor)
el postre = *dessert*

check**point** 4

1   What's the Spanish for *I beg your pardon*?

2   If you think you're getting blank looks, how can you check whether you're making sense?

3   What small word means *how/what* and can be used with a noun or an adjective to comment?

4   How would you ask how to say *crisis* in Spanish?

5   What do you add to **realidad** to say *in fact*?

6   Is **¡Qué lío!** an expression of pleasure or irritation?

7   Rearrange these words to form a sentence you might need in a restaurant: **alergia trigo y los lácteos tengo a al productos**

8   **Des-** in **desafortunado/a** and **desagradable** show that they mean the opposite of **afortunado/a** and **agradable**. What do you think these verbs mean: **desarmar, desvestirse, deshacer, deshumanizar**?

9   Class the following as positive or negative: **¡Qué casualidad! ¡Qué asco! ¡Qué alegría! ¡Qué lástima!**

10 How do you ask somebody if they would mind explaining?

11 Which of these are not used to say *well*? **bueno, aún, todavía, entonces, pues, total**

12 You come across **salmorejo** on a Spanish menu. How would you ask what it means?

13 What's *for example* in Spanish?

14 What do you add to **Este suceso es .... triste** to mean *This event is rather sad*?

15 If someone you're dining with says **Paguemos a medias**, what would you be expected to do?

16 Which of these means *I'm hungry*: **Tengo mala leche, Tengo sed** or **Tengo hambre**?

17 How would you say *Lucky you!* to a close friend?

18 Fill the gaps to say. *How good it smells! It's making my mouth water.* **¡Qué .... huele! .... me hace la boca agua.**

19 Which one of these could you drink: **cazuela, coliflor** or **calimocho**?

20 How do you say that something's on the tip of your tongue?

cinco
what's happened

A real conversation is unpredictable: it may at times be confined to the here and now but is more likely to veer comfortably between the present, past and future. When it comes to talking about what's just happened to you or recounting an anecdote, then the past tenses are essential.

English and Spanish have different ways of referring to events in the past. English relies heavily on words such as *has, have, was, were* and *did*. Using *to play* as an example, you can say *I played, I did not play, I have played, I have been playing, I was playing, I would (often) play*. Spanish is a bit more straightforward, with all these conveyed via:

● **he jugado** the perfect tense
● **jugué** the preterite tense
● **jugaba** the imperfect tense

The key to choosing the right one is to focus on the context in which each one is used, rather than on the words you would use in English.

Being able to talk about the past brings a whole new dimension to your Spanish, and it's easy to practise. Every so often you can say to yourself what you've been doing, preferably out loud; every day spend a few minutes writing a journal. You'll be using the same structures over and over, and your vocabulary will expand exponentially as you look up any new words you need.

what you've been doing

To talk about what you did, have done or have been doing, you use the perfect tense, which is in two parts, just like *have + played* in English.

1   present tense of **haber** *to have*

yo	he	nosotros/as	hemos
tú	has	vosotros/as	habéis
usted	ha	ustedes	han
él/ella	ha	ellos/ellas	han

2   + past participle. In English this often ends in -*ed*, e.g. *worked*, *watched*, *sneezed*; in Spanish you change the ending of the infinitive:

-ar → -ado	**trabaj**ar *to work*	**trabaj**ado *worked*
-er → -ido	**vend**er *to sell*	**vend**ido *sold*
-ir → -ido	**viv**ir *to live*	**viv**ido *lived*

The perfect tense is used to talk about things that you have done within a period of time that is still going on, such as **hoy** *today*, **este año** *this year*, **esta semana** *this week* or at a time close to the present, such as **esta mañana** *this morning*, **últimamente** *lately*.

He **perd**ido mi cartera y mis llaves. *I have lost my wallet and my keys.*
Esta mañana no he **pod**ido acceder a mis correos electrónicos.
I haven't been able to access my emails this morning.
¿Has **llam**ado a tu madre? *Have you rung your mum?*
Ha **cambi**ado de opinion. *He's changed his mind.*
¿Has **prob**ado alguna vez el gazpacho? *Have you ever tried gazpacho?*
Alguien ha **dej**ado un mensaje. *Someone (has) left a message.*
Eduardo me ha **ayud**ado. *Eduardo has helped me/has been helping me.*
Hemos **com**ido demasiado. *We've eaten too much.*
¿Habéis **visit**ado alguna vez el museo Guggenheim en Bilbao? *Have you ever visited the Guggenheim museum in Bilbao?*
Finalmente, han **solucion**ado el problema con la tarjeta de crédito. *At last they've sorted out the problem with the credit card.*

To say you have *just* done something, you can use the present tense of **acabar de** + an infinitive: **Acabo de comer.** *I have just eaten.*
Acabo de recibir tu mensaje. *I have just received your message.*
Acabamos de visitar la Alhambra. ¡Qué maravilla! *We've just visited the Alhambra. What a wonderful place!*

irregular past participles

Just as English has irregular past participles such as *eat* → *eaten, catch*
→ *caught, freeze* → *frozen*, so too does Spanish. Spanish **-ar** verbs have
regular past participles, but many common **-er** and **-ir** verbs don't, e.g:

abrir *to open*	**abierto** *open*
decir *to say*	**dicho** *said*
descubrir *to discover*	**descubierto** *discovered*
escribir *to write*	**escrito** *written*
hacer *to do, to make*	**hecho** *done, made*
morir *to die*	**muerto** *dead*
poner *to put, to place*	**puesto** *put, placed*
romper *to break*	**roto** *broken*
resolver *to solve*	**resuelto** *solved*
ver *to see*	**visto** *seen*
volver *to return*	**vuelto** *returned*

Ya lo he hecho. *I've already done it.*
Aún/Todavía no lo he hecho. *I haven't done it yet.*
Recientemente he abierto **una nueva cuenta corriente.** *I've recently opened
a new current account.*
¿Han descubierto **la causa?** *Have they found out the cause?*
Perdón, he roto **un vaso.** *Sorry, I've broken a glass.*
He escrito **la carta de agradecimiento.** *I've written the thank you letter.*
¿Dónde has puesto **la cafetera?** *Where have you put the coffee maker?*
Ha sido **una excursión maravillosa. Hemos** visto **focas, delfines y una
enorme ballena**. *It's been a great trip. We've seen seals, dolphins and a huge
whale.*
Ha muerto **de un infarto.** *He has died of a heart attack.*
¡Dicho y hecho! *No sooner said than done.*

Past participles only change when they're being used as
adjectives, when the endings change like any other adjective
ending in **-o**.
La puerta está abierta. *The door's open.*
Todas las gallinas están muertas. *All the chickens are dead.*
¿Por qué están rotos estos platos? *Why are these plates broken?*

what you did

In contrast to the perfect tense, the preterite is used to talk about events and actions that have been completed. Compare these pairs of sentences:

He hecho la compra. *I've done the shopping.*
Hice **la compra ayer.** *I did the shopping yesterday.*
¿Has hablado con el guía? *Have you spoken to the guide?*
¿Hablaste **con el guía anoche?** *Did you speak to the guide last night?*

The preterite has regular patterns of verb endings.

hablar	hablé *I spoke*	hablamos *we spoke*
to speak	hablaste *you spoke*	hablasteis *you spoke*
	habló *he, she, you (**Ud.**) spoke*	hablaron *they, you (**Uds.**) spoke*

Regular -er and -ir verbs have the same preterite endings:

comer	comí *I ate*	comimos *we ate*
to eat	comiste *you ate*	comisteis *you ate*
	comió *he, she, you (**Ud.**) ate*	comieron *they, you (**Uds.**) ate*

vivir	viví *I lived*	vivimos *we lived*
to live	viviste *you lived*	vivisteis *you lived*
	vivió *he, she, you (**Ud.**) lived*	vivieron *they, you (**Uds.**) lived*

Ayer limpié la casa y llamé a la agencia para reservar el viaje. *Yesterday I cleaned the house and called the agency to book the trip.*
El martes pasado hablé con María y quedamos en vernos el domingo. *Last Tuesday I talked to María and we arranged to see each other on Sunday.*
Alquilamos un coche y viajamos por toda Andalucía. *We rented a car and we travelled all over Andalusia.*
No quedaron ayer con María porque terminaron de trabajar muy tarde. *They didn't meet with María yesterday because they finished work very late.*
El viaje me costó más de cinco mil euros. *The trip cost me more than 5,000 euros.*
Salimos a las siete de la mañana, almorzamos a las dos y no llegamos hasta las ocho de la tarde. *We left at seven in the morning, had lunch at two and didn't arrive until eight in the evening.*
La fiesta duró hasta el amanecer. *The party lasted until dawn.*
Comimos en uno de los chiringuitos de la playa. *We ate in one of the beach restaurants.*
Por la tarde jugaron al fútbol. Juan marcó un gol/un golazo. *They played football in the afternoon. Juan scored a goal/a brilliant goal.*

finding out about someone's past

To find out about specific events in someone's past, you'll be asking questions that largely involve the preterite tense:

¿Te casaste muy joven? *Did you get married very young?*
¿Compraste esta casa hace mucho tiempo? *Did you buy this house a long time ago?*

You can also start with a question word (pages 26–27).
¿Dónde os conocisteis? *Where did you meet?*
¿Cuándo os casasteis? *When did you two get married?*
¿Dónde se conocieron Pedro y Penélope? *Where did Pedro and Penelope meet?*
¿Por qué decidiste venir a Madrid? *Why did you decide to come to Madrid?*

You use the preterite of **nacer** to talk about when and where people were born.
¿Dónde naciste? *Where were you born?*
¿Dónde nació Alejandro? *Where was Alejandro born?*
¿Dónde nacieron tus hijos? *Where were your children born?*
Nací en Córdoba. *I was born in Córdoba.*
Mi mujer es inglesa: nació en York. *My wife is English: she was born in York.*
Mi hija nació en Andalucía en el año dos mil. *My daughter was born in Andalusia in the year 2000.*
Mis bisabuelos eran irlandeses. Nacieron en Limerick, pero emigraron a Australia en mil novecientos veinte. *My great-grandparents were Irish but they emigrated to Australia in 1920.*
Nací en Madrid, pero pasé toda mi infancia y juventud en Granada. *I was born in Madrid but I grew up in/spent my childhood and my youth in Granada.*
Nací en Valencia, pero viví muchos años en Argentina. *I was born in Valencia but I lived for many years in Argentina.*

Have a go at saying where you were born and where you grew up, then do the same for a few members of your family.

To say the year in Spanish, you often group the numbers in a different way from English. Instead of *nineteen sixty-eight*, for example, you say *one thousand, nine hundred and sixty-eight*: **mil novecientos sesenta y ocho**.
in 1936 **en mil novecientos treinta y seis**, *in 2000* **en el año dos mil**, *in 2017* **en dos mil diecisiete**

sharing experiences

Chatting about what you've been doing is a staple part of conversation, for which you'll need verbs like **ir** to go, **ser** and **estar** to be, **andar** to walk, to go and **tener** to have – all of which are irregular in the preterite.

was and went

Surprisingly, **ser** and **ir** share the same irregular preterite forms.
fui I was, I went
fuiste you were, you went
fue he/she, it was; you (**Ud.**) were; he/she, it went; you (**Ud.**) went
fuimos we were, we went
fuisteis you were, you went
fueron they were, you were (**Uds.**); they went, you went (**Uds.**)

dar to give behaves as though it were an -ir verb: **yo di, tú d**iste etc.
decir to say: dije, dijiste, dijo, dijimos, dijisteis, dijeron
hacer: hice, hiciste, hizo, hicimos, hicisteis, hicieron
The **z** in hizo keeps the th sound. Several verbs change spelling in the preterite to preserve the core sound, e.g. **jugar** to play: jugué I played but jugamos we played.

Several verbs have endings which feature -**u**-, for example:
tener: tuve, tuviste, tuvo, tuvimos, tuvisteis, tuvieron
estar: estuve, estuviste, estuvo, estuvimos, estuvisteis, estuvieron
andar: anduve, anduviste, anduvo, anduvimos, anduvisteis, anduvieron

¿Adónde fuisteis **ayer?** Where did you go yesterday?
Fuimos **a la Ciudad de las Artes y las Ciencias y después** hicimos **un recorrido por el casco antiguo.** We went to the City of the Arts and Sciences and then we did a tour of the Old Town.
¿Sabe lo que hizo **mi marido ayer?** Jugó **un partido de fútbol con los hijos de nuestros vecinos y se** hizo **daño en el tobillo. Ahora no puede caminar.** Do you know what my husband did yesterday? He played a game of football with our neighbour's children and hurt his ankle. Now he can't walk.
Le regalé **a mi madre un ramo de flores para el Día de la Madre. Me** dijo **que le** gustó **mucho y me** dio **un beso.** I gave my mum a bunch of flowers for Mother's day. She said she liked it a lot and gave me a kiss.
¿Has leído la novela Las cosas que no nos dijimos? Es muy buena. Have you read the novel The Things We Didn't Say to One Another? It's very good.

wordbank

You're going to need expressions to say **when** something happened.

anoche *last night*
ayer *yesterday*
ayer por la mañana/tarde/noche *yesterday morning/afternoon/evening*
anteayer *the day before yesterday*
el otro día *the other day*

el día anterior/antes *the day before, the previous day*
el día antes de la fiesta *the day before the party*
la semana/el mes/el año anterior *the week/month/year before*

el lunes/el sábado/el mes pasado *last Monday/Saturday/month*
la semana pasada *last week*
el pasado enero *last January*

en febrero/mayo *in February/May*
en Navidad/Semana Santa *at Christmas/Easter*
en dos mil doce *in 2012*

hace poco/un rato *a short time ago*
hace media hora/dos días *half an hour/two days ago*
hace quince días *a fortnight ago*
hace alrededor de un mes *about a month ago*
hace dos/tres/diez años *two/three/ten years ago*

 Choose half a dozen of these occasions and say out loud what you did at that time. Use the preterite and include where possible the perfect as well, e.g.

El lunes pasado fui a la piscina municipal. **Last Monday I went to the local swimming pool.**

Hace tres años decidí aprender español. No ha sido fácil, pero me gustó desde el principio. **Three years ago I decided to learn Spanish. It hasn't been easy but I liked it from the very beginning.**

In Latin America and north-western Spain, the preterite tends to be used instead of the perfect tense, whatever the context.

what you used to do

¿Dónde veraneabas **de pequeño?** *Where did you spend the summers when you were little?*

Veraneabas comes from **veranear** *to spend the summer.* The imperfect tense **-abas** ending along with **de pequeño** show that the question isn't referring to a specific event. The imperfect is the tense for what used to happen, what was happening and what carried on over a period of time.

The imperfect endings of **-ar** verbs all contain a distinctive **-b-** sound.

visitar *to visit*	**visit**aba	**visit**ábamos
	visitabas	**visit**abais
	visitaba	**visit**aban

Siempre veraneábamos **en el mismo lugar.** *We always used to spend the summer in the same place.*
Todos los años nos alojábamos **en el mismo hotel.** *We stayed at the same hotel every year.*
A menudo visitábamos **el Parque Nacional de Doñana.** *We often visited Doñana National Park.*
Mi madre siempre sacaba **muchas fotos cuando** estábamos **de vacaciones.** *My mother used to take lots of photos when we were on holiday.*
Comprábamos **queso en el mercado.** *We (always) bought cheese in the market.*
¡Escuchábamos **la radio durante horas!** *We used to listen to the radio for hours!*

 All -ar verbs are regular in the imperfect. So once you know, for example, almorzar to have lunch, bailar to dance, cenar to have dinner, merendar to have a snack/picnic, nadar to swim, pasear to go for a walk, viajar to travel, you can talk about some of the things you used to do on holiday simply by replacing the -ar with an imperfect ending. Try putting together four or five short sentences staring with De pequeño/a veraneaba ...

To keep practising the imperfect endings and boosting your vocabulary, guess what the following verbs mean and have a go at saying out loud I used to ... acompañar, calcular, comenzar, exagerar, imaginar, invitar, indicar, justificar, participar, preparar. Then, We used to ... and They used to ...

The imperfect of **-er** and **-ir** verbs sounds rather different from **-ar** verbs. Instead of **-b-**, the endings include **ía**:

comer *to eat* → **com**ía *I would eat*
salir *to go out* → **sal**ía *I used to go out*

comer *to eat*	com**ía**	com**íamos**
	com**ías**	com**íais**
	com**ía**	com**ían**
vivir *to live*	viv**ía**	viv**íamos**
	viv**ías**	viv**íais**
	viv**ía**	viv**ían**

Todos los días salía a las siete. *I left/would leave at seven o'clock every day.*
Rosario venía todos los sábados a nuestra casa. *Rosario used to come to our house every Saturday.*
Cuando ella trabajaba en Colombia, nos manteníamos en contacto por Skype o FaceTime porque nos costaba menos.
When she worked in Colombia, we used to keep in touch via Skype or FaceTime because it was cheaper.
Antes comía carne, pero ahora soy vegetariana. *I used to eat meat before but now I am vegetarian.*
No lo sabía. *I didn't know.*
Cuando vivía en España, hacía mucho turismo rural. *When I lived Spain I used to spend a lot of holidays in the countryside.*
Cuando no trabajaba, leía muchos libros. Ahora no tengo tiempo. *When I wasn't working, I read a lot of books. Now I don't have time.*

The verb **soler** *to be accustomed to* is often used in the imperfect to talk about something you used to do or did often. It is followed by a verb in the infinitive:
Solía tocar la guitarra para relajarme. *I used to play the guitar in order to relax.*
Todos los días solíamos coger el bus. *Every day we used to catch the bus.*
Solían ir de vacaciones al extranjero. *They often went on holiday abroad.*

how things were

To describe how things were or used to be, you need the imperfect of **ser** and **estar**. While **estar** is regular, the imperfect of **ser** is irregular:
era, eras, era, éramos, erais, eran

Ayer estaba muy cansado. No sé por qué. *I was really tired yesterday. I don't know why.*
Éramos cuatro. *There were four of us.*
Hace veinte años, este edificio era una escuela. *This building was a school twenty years ago.*
A veces Cristina estaba algo torpe. *Cristina used to be a bit clumsy at times.*
¿Cómo era la ciudad antes? *What was the town like before?*
Era muy elegante. *He/She/It was very elegant.*
No era grande, era así de pequeño. *It wasn't big, it was this small.*

Along with **ser**, there are only two other verbs that are irregular in the imperfect:
ir *to go*: iba, ibas, iba, íbamos, ibais, iban
ver *to see*: veía, veías, veía, veíamos, veíais, veían
¿Adónde ibas por las tardes? *Where did you go in the evenings?*
Antes veíamos la tele cada noche, pero ahora estamos todo el día con Internet. *We used to watch TV every evening but now we spend all day on the internet.*

---

word bank

Expressions such as the following are often used with the imperfect:
de niño/a, de pequeño/a *as a child, when I was little*
de joven *when I was young*

siempre *always*
nunca *never*
normalmente *usually*
raramente *rarely*

muchas veces *often*
pocas/raras veces *occasionally*
a veces *sometimes*
de vez en cuando *from time to time*
todos los días/semanas/meses *every day/week/month*
cada día/semana/año *every day/week/year*

reminiscing

When people are getting to know each other, there's usually a mutual interest in finding out about personal background.

Since you are born only the once, you use the preterite tense:
¿Dónde naciste? *Where were you born?*
Nací en Palencia. *I was born in Palencia.*

From then on, you need the imperfect.
¿Dónde vivías de pequeño? *Where did you use to live when you were little?*
Vivíamos en un pueblo muy pequeño cerca de Palencia. *We used to live in a little village near Palencia.*
No había tiendas, pero cada día venía el panadero a traer pan fresco y los miércoles íbamos a otro pueblo cercano para hacer la compra. *There were no shops but every day the baker used to come to bring fresh bread and on Wednesdays we used to go to a nearby village to do the shopping.*
Teníamos una vida muy tranquila. *We used to have a very quiet life.*
Mi padre trabajaba en la empresa familiar y mi madre cuidaba de la casa y de los hijos. *My father worked/used to work in the family business and my mother used to look after the house and the children.*
Vivíamos en una casa bastante pequeña, pero muy acogedora. *We lived in a house that was quite small but very cosy.*
Los domingos comíamos con mis abuelos, que vivían en otro pueblo a veinte kilómetros. *On Sundays we used to have lunch with my grandparents who lived in another village, 20 km away.*
Siempre estaba con mi perro, Tufi. Era mi mejor amigo. *I was always with my dog, Tufi. He was my best friend.*
Iba al colegio en autobús. Me encantaba ir al colegio. *I used to go to school by bus. I loved going to school.*
Tenía muchos amigos y los profesores eran muy amables y cariñosos. *I had many friends and the teachers were very kind and caring.*

 Think of at least six sentences in Spanish about when you were growing up.

bringing it together

You often need the preterite and the imperfect tenses in the same sentence, for example, the imperfect describes the circumstances in which something took place (preterite).

Yo tenía **veinte años cuando** conocí **a Rosi.** *I was 20 when I met Rosi.*

Ya anochecía **cuando** llegué. *It was getting dark when I arrived.*

El restaurante estaba **a tope cuando** llegamos. *The restaurant was packed when we went there.*

And within the course of even a short conversation, you'll often need to use several tenses.

¿Saliste **anoche?** *Did you go out last night?*

No, me quedé **en casa.** He tenido **un resfriado muy fuerte esta semana y** estaba **agotada.** *No, I stayed at home. I've had a bad cold this week and I was very tired.*

¿Has visto **la última película de Almodóvar?** *Have you seen the last film by Almodóvar.*

Sí, la vi **el sábado pasado. Antes me** gustaban **mucho sus películas, pero esta no me** ha gustado **mucho.** *Yes, I saw it last Saturday. I used to like his films a lot but I didn´t like this one much.*

¿Has probado **alguna vez el gazpacho?** *Have you ever tried* ***gazpacho?***

Sí, lo tomé **una vez en el sur de España.** Hacía **mucho calor y el gazpacho es perfecto para los días calurosos.** *Yes, I had it once in the south of Spain. It was very hot and* ***gazpacho*** *is perfect for hot days.*

To convey a sense of being right in the middle of doing something when something else happened, you can use the imperfect of **estar** followed by a verb ending in **-ando** (**-ar** verbs) or **-iendo** (**-er** and **-ir** verbs).

Estaba guardando el archivo cuando falló el ordenador. *I was saving the file when the computer crashed.*

¿Qué estabas haciendo cuando te llamé? *What were you doing when I called you?*

¡Estaba haciéndome un selfie y me caí! *I was taking a selfie and I fell over!*

Estaban viendo una película y no oyeron nada. *They were watching a film and heard nothing.*

saying something had taken place

In Spanish, as in English, the only difference between saying something *has* happened and *had* happened is the tense of *have*. To convey *had happened* in Spanish, you use the imperfect of **haber** + a past participle. This is called the pluperfect tense, and in English *had* is very often shortened to *'d*.

había, habías, había, habíamos, habíais, habían

Me había olvidado **de echar gasolina.** *I had forgotten to get petrol.*
Ya había preguntado **por qué.** *I'd already asked why.*
¿Habías leído el libro antes de ver la película? *Had you read the book before seeing the film?*
Estaba cansado porque no había dormido **bien.** *He was tired because he hadn't slept well.*
No había viajado **en autobús antes porque tarda más.** *I hadn't travelled by bus before because it takes longer.*
Ya habían pagado **el billete.** *They had already paid the fare.*

---

buses, camels and gondolas

Spanish is spoken in 19 of Latin America's 21 countries but there are a number of variations in the way common words are used and sometimes in the words themselves. The humble bus, for instance, which in Spain is **un autobús** (**un autocar** is *a coach*) has many other names across the continent.

In Argentina it is **un colectivo**, now being replaced by more modern **omnibuses**. Peru's capital, Lima, has fleets of minibuses called **micros**, while in Mexico the word to use is **un camión**, *a lorry* in Spain.

Panama City's **diablos rojos** *red devils* are brightly painted, dramatically decorated and often madly driven. In Santo Domingo, Puerto Rico, Cuba (and the Canary Islands) the buses have the entertaining name of **guagua** (pronounced *wa wa*) or **guagüita**, which are rivalled by Chile's **góndolas** and Cuba's weird-looking articulated **camellos**.

A word of warning if you're catching a bus in Argentina: the expression **coger un bus** means to catch a bus in Spain, but in Argentina and other countries in Latin America **coger** means something very rude, so you should use the verb **tomar** instead.

talking the talk

Javier	¿Qué tal el fin de semana?
Isabel	Genial. Fuimos a la costa. Cuando llegamos, hacía un tiempo espléndido. Los niños jugaron y se bañaron mientras Ana y yo leíamos, charlábamos y nos relajábamos.
Javier	¿Qué niños? ¿Y quién es Ana?
Isabel	Mi hermana. Tiene dos hijos ... ¿Y tú, qué hiciste?
Javier	Pues yo, jugué un partido de fútbol con mi vecino y sus hijos, pero mi vecino se hizo daño en el tobillo. ¡El partido duró solo cinco minutos! Despúes ... nada interesante ... limpié la casa, hice la compra, fui al gimnasio, en fin, todo lo que no había hecho durante la semana. Estaba muy cansado, ¿sabes?
Isabel	No me sorprende. Además, trabajaste muchas horas la semana pasada, ¿no?
Javier	Es cierto. Pero, lo bueno es que acabo de terminar el proyecto del que te hablé antes.
Isabel	¡Qué alivio!
Isabel	Dime, ¿has visitado alguna vez el Museo Guggenheim en Bilbao?
Javier	Lo visité con mi familia cuando abrió en 1997. No recuerdo nada.
Isabel	Hablas poco de tu familia. ¿Naciste en Castilla y León? ¿Pasaste toda tu infancia allí?
Javier	Hasta que me casé.
Isabel	¡Estás casado! No lo sabía.
Javier	Estaba casado. Mi exmujer cambió de opinión y se casó con mi otro hermano.
Isabel	¿Tu mujer se ha casado con tu hermano? ¡Ay Dios mío! ¡Ay!
Javier	Vamos.

verb practice 3

1 Write the correct part of these verbs in the imperfect tense.

  a **querer** to want   **tú** ....

  b **tener** to have   **nosotros/as** ....

  c **ir** to go   **usted** ....

  d **bañarse** to bathe   **ellos/as** ....

  e **hacer** to do   **yo** ....

  f **charlar** to chat   **nosotros/as** ....

  g **ser** to be   **ustedes**...................

  h **leer** to read   **vosotros/as** ....

2 Insert the correct part of **haber** to complete these sentences in the perfect tense.

  a ¿(Tú) .... llamado a tu marido?

  b La excursión a Toledo .... sido maravillosa.

  c Carola y Eduardo me .... ayudado mucho.

  d ¿Dónde .... puesto usted la botella?

  e Mis padres .... ido a las islas Canarias.

  f Yo .... escrito una carta de agradecimiento.

  g Mis amigos y yo .... comido en la cafetería.

  h ¿Quién .... roto este vaso?

  i Todos los residentes .... vuelto a sus casas.

3 The verbs in these sentences are in the perfect tense. Can you change the meaning by putting them in the preterite tense?

  a Lo he hecho.

  b Ellos han comprado un coche.

  c ¿Has pagado la cuenta?

  d Ha muerto el alcalde.

  e Hemos arreglado el problema.

4 Fill in the gaps by translating the English words in brackets, then translate the sentences.

  a .... con Juan; .... en la plaza y yo ....

    (I was, we were, fell over)

  b .... en 1964; de niña, ... en Galicia, donde sus abuelos .... un hotel-restaurante.

    (she was born, she lived, had)

  c ¿......... al pueblo donde tu madre .... a tu padre?

    (did you go, met)

1   Do you use the imperfect, the perfect or the pluperfect tense to talk about what you did/used to do when you were growing up?

2   Which two verbs share the same preterite tense?

3   What are the past participles of **prohibir** *to prohibit*, **dejar** *to leave*, **lograr** *to succeed*, **coger** *to catch*, all of them regular?

4   Which is the odd one out among these words, and why? **colectivo, autobús, camello, góndola**

5   What do you need to add to **Íbamos a Londres ...** to say *We used to go to London every week*?

6   How would you say *I've recently bought a guitar*?

7   How would you tell someone you've lost your passport and your keys?

8   And how would you say *There's been an accident in the street*?

9   What two ways can you think of to say *last night* in Spanish?

10 What's the difference between **Acabo de hacerlo** and **Solía hacerlo**? How would you change the verb endings from **yo** to **nosotros/as**?

11 What's the difference between **anteayer** and **el otro día**?

12 How do you tell someone that you met **Ana** when you were 12?

13 Rearrange these words to form a sentence: **¿leído la el antes libro de ver película habías?**

14 *To think about* (something) in Spanish is **pensar**. What's the difference in meaning between **estoy pensando** and **estaba pensando**?

15 How do you change these from the pluperfect to the perfect: **no había visto, habían llegado, ¿Habíais estado antes?, No habíamos estado nunca**?

seis
lifestyle choices

Knowing how to say what you like and enjoy — or don't — is something that comes in useful in all sorts of situations, whether you're referring to food or the weather, discussing work, sport, people, music, places, your interests or your pet hates.

Spanish expresses liking differently from English. While English uses *I like* and *I enjoy*, Spanish uses **me gusta** which literally means *is pleasing to me, pleases me*. It follows that when you like more than one thing, you need to say ***are pleasing to me***: **me gustan**.

In Spanish, you need **el/la, los/las** in front of the thing you like/dislike:
Me gusta el golf/la natación. *I like golf/swimming.*
No me gustan las arañas. *I don't like spiders.*

Like has other meanings too.
I like coffee and *I'd like a coffee* mean different things, even though they both use the word *like*. In Spanish, they're **Me gusta el café** *I like coffee* and **Quisiera/Quería un café** *I'd like a coffee*.

Like can also be translated as **como**:
como nuevo *like new*, **como en casa** *just like at home*
dormir como un lirón *sleep like a log* lit. *a dormouse*
comer como una lima *eat like a horse* lit. *a file*
hablar como un loro *talk incessantly* lit. *like a parrot*

Parecer means *to be like, to seem*: **Parece chicle** *It's like chewing gum*; and **parecerse** *to look like*: **Se parece a su padre** *He looks like his dad*.

what you do and don't like

what you like

Me gusta Madrid or **Madrid me gusta.** *I like Madrid.* lit. *Madrid is pleasing to me*
Me gusta. *I like it.*

To say you like more than one thing, **me gusta** becomes **me gustan**:
Estos pantalones me gustan. *I like these trousers.* lit. *These trousers are pleasing to me.*

We like/enjoy ... is **nos gusta/gustan**:
Nos gusta Andalucía. *We like Andalusia.*
Nos gustan los espárragos. *We like asparagus.*

... and what you don't like

No me gusta este vino. *I don't like this wine.*
La habitación no nos gusta. *We don't like the room.*
No me gustan las almejas. *I don't like clams.*

what other people like

To say what other people like, the only word that changes is **me** (see pages 162–164):
He likes and *she likes* are both **le gusta/gustan.**
Le gusta el ciclismo en carretera. *He/She enjoys road cycling.*
Le gustan las películas de aventuras. *He/She likes adventure films.*
You can add **a él** or **a ella** to make it clear whether you mean *he* or *she*.
A él/A ella le gusta el invierno. *He/She likes winter.*

They like is **les gusta/gustan**:
Les gusta la fotografía. *They enjoy photography.*
Les gustan tanto el marisco como la carne. *They like shellfish as much as meat.*

do you like ...?

You use **te, le, os, les,** depending on who you're talking to.
¿Te gusta la vela? *Do you like sailing?* **(tú)**
¿Os gustan las ostras? *Do you like oysters?* **(vosotros/as)**
¿No te/le/os/les gusta la comida picante? *Don't you like spicy food?*

what you like doing

When saying what you like doing, English can use an infinitive or a verb ending in *-ing*, but Spanish always uses an infinitive:

Me gusta viajar. *I enjoy travelling. I like to travel.*
Me gusta correr maratones. *I like running marathons.*
No me gusta perder el tiempo. *I don't like wasting time.*
Nos gusta estar al aire libre. *We enjoy being outdoors.*
Pero no nos gusta pasar mucho tiempo en la playa. *But we don't like spending much time on the beach.*

¿Te gusta escuchar música? *Do you enjoy listening to music?*
¿No te gusta cantar? *Don't you like singing?*
¿Le gusta bailar? *Do you enjoy dancing?*
¿Os gusta ir a conciertos? *Do you like going to concerts?*

You'll often hear **a mí me gusta** for *I like*. The added **a mí** gives emphasis, and it works whether you're talking about liking a thing or doing something.

A mí no me gusta este plato. *I don't like this dish.*
A mí me gustan las personas que dicen lo que piensan. *I like people who say what they think.*
A mí me gusta pescar. *I like fishing.*

In the same way, you add **a nosotros/as** before **nos**, **a ti** before **te**, **a usted/él/ella** before **le**, **a vosotros/as** before **os** and **a ustedes/ellos/ellas** before **les**.

A nosotros nos gusta acampar en el campo. *We like camping in the countryside.*
A mí me gusta el golf, pero a ella no. *I like golf but she doesn't.*
¿A ti te gusta el golf? *Do you like golf?*
A ellas les gusta correr descalzas. *They* (f) *like running barefoot.*

You also need **a** before a named or specific person.

A Mateo le gusta el Atlético de Madrid. *Mateo likes Atlético de Madrid.*
A mi mujer no le gustan los caracoles. *My wife doesn't like snails.*

El gusto means *taste* as in one of the five senses or taste in clothes, etc:
Tiene muy buen gusto para la ropa. *He/she has a very good taste in clothes.*
For taste when it refers to flavour use **el sabor**: **No me gusta el sabor del pescado.** *I don't like the taste of fish.*

adding nuance

Slotting words like **mucho** *a lot, very much* or **tanto** *so much* into a sentence adds nuance or depth to what you're saying. It's simple to do: since they're adverbs, there's nothing about them to change. They're especially useful when you're talking about what you like, since *I like* and *I don't like* can sound rather stark on their own.

Me gusta mucho Enrique Iglesias. *I like Enrique Iglesias very much.*
Estos me gustan mucho. *I like these a lot.*
Me gusta tanto esquiar. *I like skiing so much.*
Me gusta bastante mi trabajo. *I quite/rather like my job.*
A nosotros nos gusta muy poco el campo. *We're not at all fond of the countryside.*

A ella le gustan muchísimo las montañas. *She really likes the mountains.*
A él le gusta mucho madrugar/levantarse temprano. *He really likes getting up early.*

¿Os gusta de verdad? *Do you truly/really like it?*
Nos gusta sinceramente. *We truly/really like it.*
La playa les gusta un montón a los chicos. *The little ones just love the beach.* lit. *The little ones like the beach a heap.*
Le gusta el chocolate con locura. *She adores chocolate.* lit. *She likes chocolate like mad.*

words of love

Querer means *to love* – but only when you're talking about people.
Quiero a mi familia. *I love my family.*
Te quiero. *I love you.*
No me quieres, ¿verdad? *You don't love me, do you?*
You don't use **querer** to say you love coffee or fruit or doing something; for those you need **me gusta (muchísimo).**

An alternative way of saying you love something or doing something is **me encanta**. It works in exactly the same way as **me gusta:**
Me encanta la música cubana. *I love Cuban music.*
Me encantan los cuadros de Miró. *I love Miró's pictures.*
Nos encanta observar los pájaros en el parque. *We love watching the birds in the park.*
A los niños les encanta la playa. *The little ones love the beach.*

love and hate

Like most languages, Spanish has colourful ways of expressing likes and dislikes.

You can use **me chifla(n)** which literally means *I absolutely adore, I love, I'm nuts about*.
¡Me chifla tu nuevo look! *I adore your new look!*
Me chiflan las patatas bravas. *I love patatas bravas.*

Flipar means *to go crazy about, to be nuts about*.
Me flipa este pub. *I'm crazy about this (night)club.*
¡Guay! ¡Flipante! ¡Qué chulo! or **¡Es chulo!** all mean *Super! Great! Cool!*

If you don't like something, on the other hand, use **no me hace(n) mucha gracia, no me va(n)** or, more emphatically, **me vuelve(n) loco/a**:
No me hace mucha gracia el ajo. *I don't get on with garlic.*
No me van los otros. *I'm not keen on the other ones.*
Me vuelven loco/a los nuevos vecinos. *The new neighbours are driving me nuts.*
Me vuelve loco/a also has the positive meaning *I'm nuts about*:
Esta canción de Juanes me vuelve loco/a. *I'm nuts about this song by Juanes.*

You emphasise the things you ***don't*** like with words like **no ... para nada** or **de ninguna manera** *not at all*. Unlike English, Spanish can use two negative words in the same sentence: **no ... nunca** *never,* **no ... nadie** *nobody*.
No me gusta para nada lavar los platos. *I can't stand doing the washing up.*
No me gustan mucho las películas de suspense. *I don't particularly like thrillers.*
Los hospitales no me gustan para nada. *I don't like hospitals at all.*
A María no le gusta de ninguna manera esperar el autobús. *María doesn't like waiting for the bus at all.*
A mis padres no les gustan los pimientos del padrón ni por asomo. *My parents don't like padrón peppers in the slightest.*
No me gustaba tomar el sol de ninguna manera, pero ahora sí. *I didn't use to like sunbathing at all but now I do.*
Aquel restaurante no le gustaba a nadie. *Nobody liked that restaurant.*
No me han gustado nunca los aeropuertos. *I've never liked airports.*

what you liked or used to like

There are three ways of saying *I liked* in Spanish: **me gustaba, me gustó** and **me ha gustado**. They work in the same way as **me gusta**: what you like can go before or after them; **me** is replaced by **te, le, nos**, etc. to say what other people liked; **no** goes beforehand to say *didn't like*.

Me gustaba/gustaban, the imperfect tense, is used in the sense of *I used to like* (page 72):
De niño, me gustaba muchísimo leer. *When I was little, I loved reading.*
¿Te gustaba el colegio? *Did you like school?*
Me gustaba bastante, pero a veces no. *I quite liked it but sometimes not.*
Antes, no le gustaban las anchoas, pero ahora sí. *Before, he didn't use to like anchovies but now he does.*
Me gustaba tanto el olor de la hierba recién cortada. *I used to like the smell of newly cut grass so much.*

Me gustó *I liked, I enjoyed* is the preterite (page 68).
Me gustó el espectáculo de ayer. *I liked yesterday's show.*
El viaje nos gustó enormemente. *We really enjoyed the trip.*
No me gustó su actitud. *I didn't like his/her attitude.*
No le gustó su último libro. *She didn't enjoy his latest book.*

The plural of **me gustó** is **me gustaron**.
Me gustaron los edificios de la Gran Vía. *I liked the buildings on the Gran Vía.*
No nos gustaron las colas largas. *We didn't like the long queues.*

The third way of talking about what you or someone else liked is **me ha gustado**, the perfect tense, often translated as *have enjoyed* (page 66).
Me ha gustado un montón el partido. *I've really enjoyed the match.*
¿Te ha gustado la paella? *Have you enjoyed/did you enjoy the paella?*

The plural of **me ha gustado** is **me han gustado**.
Nos han gustado todas las canciones. *We've enjoyed all the songs.*
¿Os han gustado las cerezas? *Did you like the cherries?*

You can add **siempre** to say *have always liked*:
Siempre me ha gustado el ajedrez. *I've always liked chess.*
Siempre nos ha gustado esta región. *We've always liked this region.*

saying what interests you

Me interesa/interesan ... *I'm interested in ...* literally means ... *interest(s) me* and works in the same way as **me gusta/gustan**.

Me interesa la ciencia. *Science interests me.*
Su argumento me interesa mucho. *Your point interests me greatly.*
Sus teorías me interesan. *I'm interested in your theories.*
¿Te interesan los barcos? *Are you keen on boats?*
¿Le interesa el automovilismo? *Are you interested in motor racing?*
No le interesa tanto el bricolaje. *He's not all that interested in DIY.*
Les interesan los caballos. *They're interested in horses.*
A nosotros nos interesa esta región. *We're interested in this region.*
¿Os interesa ver la catedral? *Are you interested in seeing the cathedral?*
A Ana le interesa la moda. *Ana's interested in fashion.*

For things that don't interest you, you put **no** before **me interesa**:
No me interesa el patinaje. *Skating doesn't interest me/appeal to me.*
El resultado no nos interesa. *We're not interested in the result.*
A mí no me interesan los crucigramas. *Crosswords don't interest me.*
La moda no le interesa a Ana. *Ana's not interested in fashion.*

There are two main ways of saying *I was interested* in Spanish:
me interesaba/interesaban (imperfect tense):
En el colegio, me interesaban las ciencias. *At school, I was interested in science.*
Cuando éramos jóvenes, solamente nos interesaba jugar. *When we were young, we were only interested in playing.*
A ellos no les interesaba trabajar. *They weren't interested in working.*

me ha interesado/han interesado (perfect tense):
Siempre me ha interesado el fútbol/la informática. *I've always been interested in football/computing.*
Sus ideas siempre me han interesado. *I've always been interested in your ideas.*
No me han interesado nunca los juegos de apuestas. *Gambling has never interested me.*

wordbank

Use the words on these two pages to practise talking about what you like or don't like, what does and doesn't interest you. If your interests or pet hates aren't included, look them up in a dictionary and make a note of them. There are tips on using a dictionary on pages 107–109.

los deportes *sport*

el alpinismo, el montañismo *climbing, mountaineering*
las artes marciales *martial arts*
el baloncesto *basketball*
correr *running*
el esquí (de fondo) *(cross-country) skiing*
la espeleología *potholing*
el fútbol (sala) *football (five a side)*
hacer footing *jogging*
la natación *swimming*
el paracaidismo *parachuting*
el parapente *paragliding*
el patinaje *skating*
el puenting *bungee-jumping*
el senderismo *hiking*
el tenis *tennis*
la vela *sailing*
Many sports use the English word, e.g. **el bádminton, el golf, el rugby, el squash, el kitesurf, el windsurf, el yoga.**

las artes *the arts*

la música clásica/pop *classical/pop music*
la música coral/sinfónica/de cámara *choral/symphonic/chamber music*
la música alternativa *alternative music*
la música contemporánea *modern music,* most of which adopts the English words, e.g. **el rock, el jazz, el punk, el blues, el hip-hop, el rap, el tecno, la electrónica**
la ópera *opera,* **la zarzuela** *operetta*
el grupo, el conjunto *group*
el concierto *concert, gig*
el baile moderno/de salón *modern/ballroom dance*
la canción *song*

el/la cantante *singer*
el arte abstracto/conceptual *abstract/conceptual art*
la exposición, la muestra *exhibition*
la galería *gallery*
el museo *museum*
un espectáculo *show, performance*
el espectáculo en vivo *live performance*
el cine *cinema*
el teatro *theatre*
la telenovela *soap opera*
el/la protagonista *leading actor/actress, star*
el reparto, el elenco *cast*
el actor/la actriz *the actor/actress*

In Spanish, unlike in English, you use **el**, **la**, **los** or **las** before a noun used in a general sense.
Me encanta el fútbol. *I love football.*
Me gustan la fruta y las verduras. *I like fruit and vegetables.*
Todos los fines de semana juego al baloncesto. *Every weekend I play basketball.* (**al** = **a** + **el**)
A mi hijo no le hacen mucha gracia las espinacas. *My son doesn't get on with spinach.*

las tareas domésticas *household jobs*
cuidar del/el jardín *to garden*
hacer bricolaje *to do DIY*
tirar la basura *empty the rubbish*
hacer la compra *to do the food shopping*
lavar *to wash* **los platos** *the dishes*
arreglar, ordenar *to tidy up, to clear up*
cargar/descargar *to load/unload;* **llenar/vaciar** *to fill/to empty*
      la lavadora *the washing machine*
      el lavaplatos, el lavavajillas *the dishwasher*
limpiar el horno/las ventanas *to clean the oven/the windows*
pasar la aspiradora *to vacuum*
reciclar *to recycle*
tender la ropa *to hang out the washing*
planchar *to iron*
cambiar las sábanas *to change the sheets*

expressing a preference

Prefiero caminar. *I prefer to walk/walking.*
Prefiero no ir solo/a. *I'd rather not go on my own.*
Yo prefiero ir en coche: es más rápido. *I'd rather go by car: it's quicker.*
Prefiero este bar a aquel. *I prefer this bar to that one.*
¿Cuál prefieres? *Which do you prefer?*
Prefiero mi viejo smartphone. *I like my old smartphone better.*
¿Qué deporte te gusta más? *Which sport do you like more/prefer?*

Preferir *to prefer* belongs to a group of verbs that have an internal spelling change (page 171). An extra **-i-** is added in the present tense except for **nosotros/as** and **vosotros/as**.
Paco prefiere el café descafeinado. *Paco prefers decaffeinated coffee.*
Prefieren el té con limón. *They prefer tea with lemon.*
Preferimos ir en primavera. *We prefer to go in spring.*
¿Cuál preferís? *Which do you like best?*

mejor *better*

As in English, **mejor** *better* can be an adjective or an adverb. When it's an adjective, i.e. when the meaning is *more good*, it changes to **mejores** in the plural.
Este de aquí es mejor: es menos voluminoso. *This one's better: it's less bulky.*
He recibido dos ofertas mejores. *I've received two better offers.*
La escuela figura entre las mejores del mundo. *The school is among the best in the world.*
Hoy estoy mejor – hace menos calor. *I feel better today – it's not as hot.*
Los niños también se sienten mejor. *The children feel better too.*
¿Cuál funciona mejor? *Which one works better/best?*

preferido/a *favourite*

Vivaldi es mi compositor preferido. *Vivaldi's my favourite composer.*
Mi jugador preferido de la selección es ... *The player I like best in the national team is ...*
Sevilla es mi ciudad preferida. *Seville is my favourite city.*
Aquí puedes ver mis sitios preferidos. *Here are my favourite sites.*

talking the talk

Isabel	¿Te gusta esta música?
Javier	En realidad, no me va mucho el jazz.
Isabel	¿Quién es el cantante que más te gusta? ¿Qué tipo de música prefieres?
Javier	A mí, David Bowie. Sus canciones son muy chulas.
Isabel	A mí me chiflan las canciones de Diego el Cigala, pero en realidad, no conozco mucho la música pop y rock. Yo prefiero más la música clásica. Mi compositor preferido es Albéniz. ¿Quizás conoces su *Suite española*?
Javier	No lo conozco bien.
Daniela	Es exquisito ... Me encanta.
Javier	Hola Daniela. ¿Qué tal?
Daniela	Bien, gracias ... ¿Habéis visto a Ángel?
Isabel	Perdonad, ahora mismo vuelvo.
Daniela	Entonces Javier, ¿qué te interesa hacer? ¿Te gustan los deportes?
Javier	Me gustan muchísimo.
Daniela	¿Qué deporte te gusta más?
Javier	Sobre todo el fútbol. ¡Qué chulo el partido de esta tarde! ... Pero me chiflan también las artes marciales. Y la vela.
Daniela	A mí también me gusta la vela. Le interesa a toda mi familia. Mi hermano pequeño y mi primo fueron campeones de España en el año dos mil quince.
Javier	¡Vaya! ¡No me digas! ¡Qué logro!
Isabel	Daniela, Ángel te busca.
Daniela	¡Hasta luego!

ahora mismo vuelvo = *I'll be right back*

checkpoint 6

1   Which is the odd one out and why: **el golf, el fútbol, el baloncesto, la natación, el tenis**?

2   How would you say in Spanish: *We really like the room*?

3   If **¿Le gustan los videojuegos?** means *Does he like computer games?*, what's the Spanish for *Does she like computer games?* and *Do they like computer games?*

4   How do you tell somebody in Spanish that you don't like skiing?

5   What's the opposite of **Me chiflan las telenovelas** *soap operas*?

6   How do you say *He/She talks incessantly* in Spanish?

7   Would you use **me gustaba** or **me ha gustado** while commenting on a wine you've just tasted?

8   What's the Spanish for *favourite* when used to talk about wines, regions, museums, music, films and photos?

9   How would you ask someone you call **tú** if he or she likes cooking?

10 The three versions of *you prefer* are **prefiere, preferís** and **prefieres**. Decide which goes with **tú**, which with **usted** and which with **vosotros/as**.

11 Give two ways of saying *They love running*.

12 Give two phrases that could go after **no me gusta** to say that you really don't like something.

13 What's the word that needs to be added to .... **me ha interesado el bricolaje** to mean *I've always been interested in DIY*?

14 What's the Spanish for *He's not interested in your ideas*?

15 Fill the gap so that **Este restaurante es ....** means *This restaurant is better*?

16 These are the words used with **me gusta** in **una encuesta** *a survey*. Put them in order, starting with the least favourable: **mucho, bastante, poco, de ninguna manera, muchísimo, con locura, muy poco**

17 How would you tell someone that you don't much enjoy getting up early, you really hate DIY, and that you prefer travelling?

siete
making plans

Spanish-speaking peoples embrace their celebrations with enthusiasm, starting on 6th January with **la fiesta de los Reyes Magos** or **el Día de Reyes** *Day of the Three Kings*, who bring presents to children. The season of **el Carnaval** follows in February, a time of partying until **el martes de Carnaval** *Shrove Tuesday* heralds **la Cuaresma** *Lent*. This lasts until **la Pascua** *Easter*, which is the culmination of **la Semana Santa** *Holy Week*. Other significant religious festivals are **la fiesta de la Asunción de la Virgen** on 15th August and **el Día de Todos los Santos** *All Saints' Day* on the 1st November, before **la Navidad** *Christmas* and **la Nochevieja** *New Year's Eve*.

In addition, there are national holidays on **el Día del Trabajo** *Labour Day* on 1st May, **la Fiesta Nacional de España** *Spain's National Day* on 12th October and regional days of celebration, not to mention scores of colourful local fiestas, amongst which are Valencia's **las Fallas, La Tomatina** and the bull running of **San Fermines**.

Feast days are celebrated in style, with family, food and drink playing a central role. If you're invited to a traditional celebration, it's worth making sure you know how to accept or to decline politely and to wish people a happy day.

when?

The days of the week, the date and the time of day are all necessary for making arrangements.

lunes *Monday*
martes *Tuesday*
miércoles *Wednesday*
jueves *Thursday*
viernes *Friday*
sábado *Saturday*
domingo *Sunday*

The Spanish way to say *on* a particular day or days is either **el** or **los**:
No puedo venir el jueves: tengo clases todos los jueves. *I can't come on Thursday: I have classes every Thursday.*
Nos vemos el sábado. *See you on Saturday.*
Los domingos no hay nadie. *There's nobody there on Sundays.*

enero *January*	**julio** *July*
febrero *February*	**agosto** *August*
marzo *March*	**septiembre** *September*
abril *April*	**octubre** *October*
mayo *May*	**noviembre** *November*
junio *June*	**diciembre** *December*

Spanish uses **el** for dates, too, and there's no additional word for *on*.
Nací el doce de octubre. *I was born on 12th October.*
El Día del Trabajo se celebra el primero/el uno de mayo. *Labour Day is celebrated on 1st May.*

bridges and aqueducts

When one of Spain's festive days falls on a Tuesday or a Thursday, many working people take the Monday or Friday off to make a long weekend. The phrase to describe this is **hacer puente**, literally: *to make the bridge*.

Occasionally, there's **un día festivo** on both the Tuesday and the Thursday, in which case the canny employee will take the whole week off, effectively bridging both bank holidays and creating **el acueducto**.

what time?

When answering **¿cuándo?** *when?* or **¿a qué hora?** *at what time?* you need *at* before the time: **a, a la** or **a las**. **En punto** means *on the dot, precisely*.

a **mediodía/medianoche**	*at midday/midnight*
a la **una**	*at one o'clock*
a las **dos en punto**	*at two o'clock on the dot*
a las **ocho y cuarto**	*at a quarter past eight*
a las **diez y media**	*at half past ten*
a las **tres menos cuarto**	*at a quarter to three*
a las **veintitrés horas**	*at 23.00, at 11 p.m.*
a las **nueve treinta**	*at 09.30*
a las **cuatro y cuarenta**	*at 04.40*

El próximo vuelo sale a las catorce cincuenta horas. *The next flight leaves at 14.50.*

A straightforward way to make a date is to use **nos vemos** *see you/we'll meet* followed by a time, day or date.
Nos vemos mañana a las diez. *See you at ten o'clock tomorrow.*
Nos vemos a las siete de la tarde. *See you at seven this evening.*
Nos vemos a las cinco de la tarde en punto. *We'll meet at 5 p.m. on the dot.*
Entonces, nos vemos a la hora de comer/a la hora del aperitivo. *Right, see you at lunchtime/aperitif time.*

Tomorrow morning is **mañana por la mañana: Nos vemos mañana por la mañana** *See you tomorrow morning*. Similarly, you can say **por la tarde** *in the afternoon/evening* and **por la noche** *at night*. **La tarde** lasts from early afternoon to **el atardecer** *sunset*, also called **la puesta de sol**.

To confirm an arrangement, the verb **quedar** is very commonly used.
Quedamos el jueves de la semana que viene. *We're agreed on Thursday next week.*
Quedamos al final de la semana próxima. *We're going for next weekend.*
¡De acuerdo! Quedamos mañana por la tarde en la tasca de Carlos, sobre las ocho y media. *Right then! We're meeting at Carlos's tapas bar around half past eight.*

suggesting things to do

Vamos is the way to suggest going somewhere.
¡Vamos a la playa! *Let's go to the beach!*
¡Vamos de compras! *Let's go shopping!*

To say *let's* with other verbs, you use the ending **-emos** for regular **-ar** verbs, and **-amos** for regular **-er** and **-ir** verbs (page 128).
¡Tomemos un helado! *Let's have an ice cream!*
¡No nos quedemos aquí! *Let's not stay here!*
¡Compartamos las noticias! *Let's share the news!*

Also common is **¿Por qué no ...?** *Why don't ...?*
¿Por qué no vamos al teatro? Sin embargo, habrá que reservar las entradas. *Why don't we go to the theatre? We'll need to book though.*
¿Por qué no compras un lavaplatos? *Why don't you buy a dishwasher?*

¿Te apetece ...? *Do you fancy ...?* **¿Qué te parece ...?** *How about ...?* and **¿Te gustaría?** *Would you like?* are all followed by an infinitive. Te is for **tú**, and changes to **le, os** or **les** if you're using **usted, vosotros/as** or **ustedes**.

¿Te apetece ir a la fiesta del vino el domingo? *Do you fancy going to the wine festival on Sunday?*
¿Les apetece caminar un poco y tomar un helado? *Would you like to go for a little walk and have an ice cream?*

¿Qué le parece jugar al tenis? *How about a game of tennis?*
¿Qué os parece ir de compras? *How about going shopping?*
¿Te gustaría comer con nosotros el domingo que viene? *Would you care to come to us for lunch next Sunday?*
¿Os gustaría dar un paseo? *Do you fancy going for a walk?*

 Practise using *¿te apetece? ¿qué te parece?* and *¿te gustaría?* with some of the examples on the next page. Say them out loud to get used to the rhythm. Remember that if the infinitive you're using ends in -se, it's a reflexive verb, and so the -se changes to te.

¿Te apetece bañarte? Do you fancy going swimming?

wordbank

ir a la ciudad *go into town*

dar un paseo por el casco antiguo *go for a walk round the old town*

ver el castillo/la catedral *see the castle/cathedral*

visitar el museo/las tiendas/las galerías *visit the museum/shops/galleries*

ir al cine; hoy ponen ... *go to the cinema; ... is on today*

ir a la ópera/a un concierto *go to the opera/to a concert*

pasar por casa de Miguel; darle un toque a Miguel *drop in on Miguel; get in touch with Miguel*

comer una pizza *go for a pizza*

alquilar una moto/un escúter *rent a motorbike/scooter*

coger/tomar el tren de cercanías hasta ... *take the local train as far as ...*

explorar los alrededores *explore the surrounding area*

ir a la fiesta del marisco *go to the shellfish festival*

ir a la fiesta del vino *go to the wine festival*

pasear(se) por los viñedos *stroll round the vineyards*

probar los vinos/los productos locales *taste local wines/products*

montar a caballo; hay un picadero muy cerca *go riding; there are stables nearby*

subir a la colina/los acantilados *climb the hill/the cliffs*

practicar el alpinismo *go mountain climbing*

atravesar la isla a pie *walk across the island*

caminar por la playa *go for a walk along the beach*

jugar a la petanca/al voleibol *have a game of boules/volleyball*

nadar, bañarse *go swimming*

hacer una excursión en barco *go on a boat trip*

practicar la pesca de altura *go deep-sea fishing*

probar el esquí acuático *have a go at water skiing*

hacer un bautismo de buceo *have an introductory lesson at the diving school*

hacer patinaje *go skating*

hacer piragüismo/canotaje *go canoeing*

hacer rafting en aguas bravas *go white-water rafting*

Try five of the above with *¿Por qué no ...?* Then have a go at using **let's**, e.g. *¡Juguemos al voleibol!* **Let's play volleyball!**

Hacer is irregular: *¡Hagamos un picnic!* **Let's have a picnic!** *Hagamos patinaje.* **Let's go skating.**

accepting and declining politely

Thanking someone for an invitation can be formal or informal:

Le/Les agradezco sinceramente haberme/habernos invitado. *Thank you so much for inviting me/us.*

Gracias por la amable invitación. *Thank you for the kind invitation.*

Muy amable (de tu/su parte). *How kind (of you).*

yes please

Acepto ... *I accept ...*
> **... con mucho gusto.** *... with pleasure.*
> **... de buena gana.** *... gladly, willingly.*

Nos gustaría mucho. *We'd love to.*

Sin duda, claro. *Certainly, definitely.*

no thank you

¡Ojalá! *If only! I wish!*

Lo siento, pero ... *I'm sorry but ...*

No será posible. *It won't be possible.*

No podré ... *I won't be able to ...*

No sé si puedo ... *I don't know if I can ...*
> **... por motivos de trabajo.** *... for work reasons.*
> **... porque tengo un compromiso.** *... because I've got something on.*

Es una lástima, pero ... *It's a real shame but ...*

Haré todo lo posible, pero ... *I'll do my best but ...*
> **... estaré fuera de la ciudad.** *... I'll be out of town.*
> **... tenemos un compromiso.** *... we're already committed.*

Gracias, de todas formas. *Thank you anyway.*

Nos veremos otro día. *Maybe another day.*

¡Ojalá! is very useful in all sorts of situations:

¿Vienes con nosotros? *Are you coming with us?* **¡Ojalá!** *If only! I should be so lucky! Chance would be a fine thing!*

¿Ganaron ayer? *Did they win yesterday?* **¡Ojalá!** *If only! You wish!*

¿Llegaste a tiempo? *Did you get there on time?* **¡Ojalá!** *I wish!*

You'll come across **Ojalá** in many everyday examples such as:

¡Ojalá fuera cierto! *If only it were true!*

Ojalá la vida fuera tan fácil. *If only life was that easy.*

Ojalá tuviéramos más tiempo. *If only we had more time.*

offering good wishes

For specific occasions you can use **Feliz ...**
Feliz cumpleaños. *Happy birthday.*
Feliz Navidad. *Happy Christmas.*

Good wishes are often prefaced with **Que tengas/tenga**:
Que tengas una feliz Navidad. *Have a happy Christmas.*
Que tenga un buen día/vuelo/viaje. *Do have a good day/flight/journey.*

You can be more formal by starting with **Te/Le/Os/Les deseo ...** *I wish you ...*:
Le deseo una buena estancia. *I wish you an enjoyable stay.*
Te deseo una feliz fiesta. *I hope you have an enjoyable party.*
Os deseamos una feliz Navidad. *Our best wishes for Christmas.*

On an everyday basis, you'll hear the following.
¡Enhorabuena! *Congratulations!*
¡Mejórate/Mejórese pronto! *Get well soon!*
¡Suerte! ¡Buena suerte! *Good luck!*
¡Salud! *Cheers!*
¡Diviértete!/¡Diviértase! *Have fun!*
¡Que lo pases/pase bien! ¡Pásalo bien!/¡Páselo bien! *Have fun!* **(tú/usted)**
To return good wishes, you say **¡Igualmente!** *You too!*

saying thank you

Gracias. *Thank you. Thanks.*
Muchas/Muchísimas gracias. *Thank you very/so much.*

You use **por** to thank someone **for** something/**for** doing something.
Muchas gracias por el regalo. Sois muy generosos. *Thanks very much for the present. You're really generous.*
Mil gracias por la ayuda. Te debo una gorda. *Thanks so much for your help. I owe you big time.*
Gracias por todo. Ha sido un día/una tarde estupendo/a. *Thanks for everything. It's been a wonderful day/evening.*
Gracias por haber venido. *Thank you for coming, having come.*

Sometimes you want your thanks to sound particularly enthusiastic.
No sé cómo agradecértelo. *I don't have the words to thank you.* **(tú)**
No sé cómo agradecérselo. *I don't have the words to thank you.* **(usted)**
Gracias de nuevo. Lo he pasado genial. *Thanks again. I've had a ball.*
Mil gracias. Me he divertido mucho. *Thank you so much. I've really enjoyed myself.*

talking about the future

Spanish has a future tense, which equates to *I will/shall do something.*
Its endings are simply added to the infinitive of all regular verbs.

yo	-é	nosotros/as	-emos
tú	-ás	vosotros/as	-éis
usted	-á	ustedes	-án
él/ella	-á	ellos/ellas	-án

contestar *to reply*: **contestar**é *I will reply*; **contestar**án *they will reply*
abrir *to open*: **abrir**ás *you will open*; **abrir**emos *we will open*
traer *to bring*: **traer**á *he/she will bring*; **traer**éis *you will bring*

The future of **hacer** *to do, to make* is irregular: **haré, harás, hará** etc.
Many other verbs don't quite follow the regular pattern but are still
recognisable: **tener** *to have*: **tendré** *I will have*; **venir** *to come*: **vendré** *I
will come*; **querer** *to want*: **querré** *I will want*; **poder** *to be able*: **podré** *I
will be able to*; **poner** *to put*: **pondré** *I will put*; **decir** *to say*: **diré** *I will say*

Talking about the future is very similar in Spanish and English, with both
the present and the future tense in common use.
Vuelven al colegio dentro de una semana. *They go back to school in a
week.*
En septiembre mi hijo empezará a ir al colegio. *In September my son
will start school.*
Hay una reunión a las once. *There's a meeting at 11 o'clock.*
Habrá una reunión a las once. *There will be a meeting at 11 o'clock.*
Si hay un retraso, te llamaré. *If there's a delay, I'll call you.*
Lo haré si puedo. Lo haré lo mejor posible. *I'll do it if I can. I'll do my
best.*
**Te mandaré un mensaje de texto/un WhatsApp para confirmar
nuestra cita.** *I'll send you a text/WhatsApp to confirm our date.*

> Both languages also talk about the future with the verb *to go:* English
> uses *going to,* while Spanish uses the present tense of *ir:* **voy, vas, va,
> vamos, vais, van,** and adds **a** before the following infinitive.
> **No voy a hacer nada.** *I'm not going to do anything.*
> **¿Va a llover mañana?** *Is it going to rain tomorrow?*
> **¡Vamos a divertirnos!** *We're going to have a good time!*
> **No van a perder. ¡Ya verás!** *They're not going to lose. You'll see!*

saying what you would do

Just as the future verb endings convey *will*, there are conditional endings that convey *would*. The conditional is often followed by *if* ... or *but* ..., indicating that there are conditions attached, hence the name. The conditional *would* has nothing do with the other English meaning of *would* that refers to the past and means *used to*, as in *she would sit and stare for hours*.

The conditional is very similar to the future tense in terms of structure, with these endings simply taking the place of future endings:

yo	-ía	nosotros/as	-íamos
tú	-ías	vosotros/as	-íais
usted	-ía	ustedes	-ían
él/ella	-ía	ellos/ellas	-ían

contestar *to reply*: **contestaría** *I would reply*
abrir *to open*: **abrirían** *they would open*
traer *to bring*: **traería** *I would bring*, **traerías** *you would bring*

The same verbs are irregular in the future and the conditional, e.g.
diría *I would say*, **haría** *I would do*, **podría** *I'd be able to*, **querría** *I'd want/ I'd like*, **tendría** *I would have*, **vendría** *I would come*.

¡No me atrevería! *I wouldn't dare!*
¿Preferirías el otro? *Would you prefer the other one?*
Te/Se lo agradecería mucho. *I'd be very grateful to you.*
Invitaría a María, pero está en Toledo. *He would invite María but she's in Toledo.*
Comería una pizza, pero estoy a dieta. *I'd eat a pizza but I'm on a diet.*
Diría que sí. *I would say yes.*
Sería demasiado caro. *It would be too expensive.*
¿No te gustaría quedarte aquí? *Wouldn't you like to stay here?*

> When a conditional is linked to *if* + another verb, this other verb is in the imperfect subjunctive (pages 166–169 and 174).
> **Sería maravilloso si fuera cierto.** *It would be wonderful if it were true.*
> **Iría yo si tuviera dinero.** *I would go myself if I had the money.*
> **Te esperaría si pudiera.** *I'd wait for you if I could.*

weather permitting

If you're arranging outdoor activities, you'll need to understand how to talk about **el tiempo** *the weather*.
La previsión meteorológica, el pronóstico meteorológico and **la previsión del tiempo** are all terms used for *weather forecast*.

¿Qué tiempo hará mañana? *What will the weather be like tomorrow?* **¿Cuál es la previsión (meteorológica) para los próximos días?** *What's the weather forecast for the next few days?*

Hay pronóstico de sol para el domingo. *The forecast is for sun on Sunday.*
Hay pronóstico de lluvia y vientos fuertes. *Rain and strong winds are forecast.*
Según las previsiones meteorológicas, esta tarde habrá vientos fuertes. *The forecast is for strong winds this evening.*

Beyond the official forecast, talking about the weather is as popular in Spanish-speaking countries as it is in the UK.

¡Hace buen tiempo! *What good weather!*
¡Qué tiempo tan bueno! *What glorious weather!*
Hace mal tiempo, ¿no? *Miserable weather, isn't it?*
¡Qué calor hace hoy! *It's very hot today!*
¡Hace tanto frío! *It's so cold!*
¡Hay mucho viento, un auténtico vendaval! *So windy, a real gale!*
¡Qué brisa tan suavecita! *What a beautiful breeze!*
Hoy hace bochorno, ¿verdad? *Really hot and muggy today, isn't it?*
Llueve: llueve a cántaros. *It's raining: it's pouring down.*
Esta lluvia continua me está molestando. *This non-stop rain is getting on my nerves.*

Quite a few expressions use **hace** for talking about the weather:
¿Qué tiempo hace donde estás tú? *What's the weather like where you are?*
Hace buen/mal tiempo. *It's a lovely/horrible day.*
Hace mucho calor: ¡hace un calor de mil demonios! *It's very hot: it's scorching!* lit. *the heat of a thousand demons*
Hace cuarenta grados a la sombra. *It's 40 degrees in the shade.*
Hace un poco de fresco. *It's a bit chilly.*
Aquí hace frío, hace un frío que pela. *It's cold here: it's arctic.*

Other common expressions use **hay** or **está**:

Está nublado/cubierto. *It's cloudy/overcast.*
Hay viento/neblina. *It's windy/misty.*
Hay mucha humedad. *It's very humid.*
Hay una llovizna muy fina. *There's a fine drizzle.*
Hay poca nieve este año. *There's not much snow this year.*

To talk about what the weather was like/has been like, you use the appropriate past tense of **hacer, haber** or **estar**:

La semana pasada hizo buen tiempo. *The weather was good last week.*
Había poca nieve pero las vistas eran estupendas. *There wasn't much snow but the views were terrific.*
Cuando llegamos estaba nublado, pero al poco tiempo salió el sol. *When we arrived it was cloudy but the sun soon came out*
Hacía un calor de mil demonios. *It was fiendishly hot.*
¡Cómo se ha nublado el día! *How cloudy it's got!*

weather wisdom

There are many traditional sayings and proverbs connected with Spain's weather. A pithy description of Madrid's quite extreme climate is **Nueve meses de invierno y tres de infierno** *Nine months of winter and three months of hell.*

Not so pithy is this poetic version of *Red sky at night ...*
Sol poniente en cielo grana, buen tiempo por la mañana. Cielo rojo a la alborada, cuidar que el tiempo se enfada. Lit. *Setting sun in a scarlet sky, good weather for the morning. Red sky at dawn, beware the weather getting angry.*

Other popular sayings include:
Hace un día de perros. *It's a filthy day.*
El sol de enero, poco duradero. *January sun doesn't last long.*
Hace un frío que quita el hipo. *It's bitterly cold.* lit. *It's cold enough to stop your hiccups.*
A mal tiempo, buena cara. *When it's bad weather, put on a good face.*
Animales perezosos, tiempo tormentoso. *Lazy animals, stormy weather.*

talking the talk

Javier	Hola, Sophie. ¿Te apetece ir al cine a ver *Julieta*?
Sophie	*¿Julieta?*
Javier	Es la última película de Almodóvar.
Sophie	Sí, me gustaría mucho verla.
Javier	¿Qué te parece si vamos el martes?
Sophie	Vale. El martes me va bien.
Javier	Perfecto. Quedamos en la puerta del cine a las nueve.
Javier	¿Te gustó?
Sophie	Sí, muchísimo. Siempre me parecen muy interesantes las películas de Almodóvar.
Javier	¿Te apetece comer algo? Yo tengo un poco de hambre.
Sophie	¿Por qué no?
Javier	Hay un buen bar de tapas bastante cerca de aquí.
Sophie	Genial, buena idea. Y podríamos darle un toque a Isabel.
Javier	¿Por qué no? Me dijo que está libre esta tarde.
Sophie	Le mando un WhatsApp para ver si quiere venir.
Javier	Sentémonos en la terraza del bar, hay un atardecer precioso. ... sol poniente en cielo grana, buen tiempo por la mañana.
Sophie	¿Qué has dicho? No he entendido nada.
Javier	Es una expresión española tradicional. Significa ...
Isabel	¡Hola chicos! ¡Buenas tardes! ¡Qué bonito este atardecer!, ¿verdad?

verb practice 4

1   Write the future forms of these verbs and say what they mean.

   a   contestar   tú ....
   b   ir   ellos/ellas ......
   c   tomar   vosotros/as ...
   d   durar   .... (*it*)
   e   poner   nosotros/as ...
   f   olvidar   usted ....
   g   lograr   yo ....
   h   hacer   ella ....
   i   llegar   nosotros/as ...
   j   estar   tú ....
   k   ser   yo ....
   l   haber   .... (*it*)

2   Now change them all to the conditional and say what they mean.

3   Identify these as present, past, future or conditional and say what
    they mean. If you need to refresh your memory of the tenses, see
    pages 166–174.

a	venceremos	b	querrás
c	ella ha llamado	d	estudian
e	quieres	f	cambiarían
g	preferiremos	h	preferiríamos
i	hubo	j	hago

4   Match the two halves to make sentences

a	Si tuviera dinero,	i	si tuviera su dirección.
b	Nueve meses de invierno	ii	ir a tomar una copa?
c	¿Cuál es el pronóstico	iii	y tres meses de infierno.
d	Les invitaría	iv	pero estoy a dieta.
e	Os agradezco	v	para la próxima semana?
f	Comería una pizza,	vi	compraría un coche.
g	¿Qué te parece	vii	habernos invitado.

checkpoint 7

1   Which are the two days on either side of **viernes** and the three months before **agosto**?

2   What's the difference in meaning between **Nos vemos el día once** and **Nos vemos a las once**?

3   What do you add to **Que tengas un buen ....** to wish someone well on a journey, on a flight and for the rest of the day?

4   Using **apetece**, how would you invite two friends to go for a walk round the old town?

5   Which one of these are you unlikely to use when accepting an invitation: **con mucho gusto, de buena gana, es una lástima, sin duda**?

6   What does **Quedamos el jueves** mean?

7   In reply to good wishes, how do you say *The same to you*?

8   Give the dates in Spanish of **el Día del Trabajo, el Día de Reyes and la Nochevieja**.

9   Rearrange these words to suggest a visit to the cinema: **vamos qué por al no cine ¿?**

10 Give the Spanish for *Let's* with **tomar, ir** and **hacer**. What do they all mean?

11 **Esta lluvia continua me .... molestando.** What's the missing word?

12 How do **hace frío** and **está nublado** change when referring to last week?

13 Complete the sentence **Quedamos el martes de la semana que ....**

14 Talking to a couple and using **vosotros**, how would you say *I'd wait for you if I could*?

15 What does **ojalá** mean?

16 How do you thank your host and say it's been a wonderful evening?

17 **¿Te apetece ir a Valencia para la fiesta de las Fallas?** Compose a text saying *I'd love to but when does the fiesta take place* (use the verb **celebrarse** for *take place*).

how to use a dictionary

A dictionary is an essential tool for language learning, allowing you to personalise phrases and talk about exactly what you choose.

There are a number of dictionaries on the internet and available as apps. Some of them are much better presented, more detailed and more user-friendly than others, and it's a case of trying a few and seeing which suits you.

In print, dictionaries come in all sizes, from tiny pocket versions to huge volumes. It's not necessarily a case of the bigger the better: a very large dictionary can be so densely packed with information that it becomes overwhelming for someone learning a language.

grammatical terms and abbreviations

As with most tools, there's a skill to using a dictionary effectively. And, because of fundamental differences between the languages, using a Spanish > English dictionary raises different issues from using the English > Spanish version.

For both, you need to understand basic terms such as adjective, adverb, noun, verb (pages 154–156), because each dictionary entry is defined by its grammatical category. This is abbreviated, and the abbreviations are very similar in both languages, with noun a notable exception: its translation can be **nombre** or **substantivo** and dictionaries abbreviate it to **n** or **s**.

art **artículo** *article*	*adj* **adjetivo** *adjective*
adv **adverbio** *adverb*	*fam* **familiar** *familiar/colloquial*
f **femenino** *feminine*	*inv* **invariable** *invariable*
irreg **irregular** *irregular*	*m* **masculino** *masculine*
n **nombre** *noun*	*pers* **persona** *person*
pl **plural** *plural*	*pp* **participio pasado** *past participle*
prep **preposición** *preposition*	*pron* **pronombre** *pronoun*
sg **singular** *singular*	*v* **verbo** *verb*
vulg **vulgar** *vulgar*	
vi/vtr **verbo intransitivo/transitivo** *intransitive/transitive verb*	

Most dictionaries include a comprehensive list of the abbreviations used.

español → inglés

Some words belong in more than one grammatical category, and a few nouns look identical but have a different gender and meaning.

---

capital *n* capital: **1** *nm* money; **2** *nf* principal town/city.

personal **I** *nm* personnel, staff: **jefe de** ~ personnel officer. **II adj** personal: **asistente** ~ personal assistant; **desarrollo** ~ personal development.

trabajo **I** *nm* work, job, employment, labour: **lugar de** ~ workplace; **búsqueda de** ~ job search; **compañero de** ~ workmate; **contrato de** ~ employment contract; **desayuno de** ~ working breakfast; **entrevista de** ~ job interview. **II** *v 1a pers sg* **trabajar** to work.

rico **I** *nm* rich man. **II adj 1** rich, wealthy; **2** delicious, tasty.

Many online dictionaries allow you to search for a word exactly as you come across it. But a traditional Spanish → English dictionary lists nouns only in the singular, adjectives with the masculine singular ending and verbs in the infinitive. This means that the word you're looking for may not appear in the dictionary exactly as you came across it.

- **Veces** and **cruces** are the plural of **vez** *time/occasion* and **cruz** *cross*, which is what you'll find listed.

- Look out for endings like **-ito**, **-illo** or **-azo**, which Spanish speakers often add to a noun instead of its usual final vowel, and which can affect spelling. **Una amiguita** *little friend* and **un golpazo** *heavy punch* come from **amiga** and **golpe**.

- Since verbs are listed in their infinitive form, ending in **-ar**, **-er** or **-ir**, you won't find a word like **trayendo**. You need to know or guess that it comes from **traer** *to bring* and then to work out that it means *bringing*.

- If you struggle with a verb, think of irregulars. **Voy** *I go* bears little resemblance to **ir** *to go*; **hizo, hará, hacen** and **hagan** all come from **hacer** *to do, to make*. A good dictionary will include common irregularities.

English → Spanish

When looking up an English word that you want to translate into Spanish, you're often faced with a range of choices. That's because many words belong in two or more categories, e.g. *sock* can be something you wear on your foot (noun) or *to hit* somebody (verb); *snipe* can be a bird (noun), to shoot or to jeer (verbs); *back* can be the rear part (noun), to support (verb) or the opposite of front (adjective).

So make sure that you select the right category. For example, if you look up the word *chuck* you'll find several Spanish options.

> **chuck I** *n* **1** *(tech)* **mandril** *m*, **portabrocas** *m*; **2** *(culin)* ~ *steak* **aguja** *f*, **paleta** *f*. **II v 1** *vtr throw* **arrojar, lanzar**; **2** *vtr* ~ *away* **descartar, tirar**; **3** *vtr break up with* **cortar**; **4** *vi vomit* **vomitar, potar** *(slang)*.

If the *chuck* you want is the thing you fit a drill bit into, then you need to look at the nouns and **el mandril** or **el portabrocas** become the obvious choice. If, though, you want to find out how to say *chuck a ball*, then you can use **arrojar** or **lanzar**. **Tirar** and **descartar** mean *to chuck away*, **cortar** *to end a relationship*, and **potar** *to throw up*.

> Spelling is, of course, critical. While *hangar* and *hanger* might sound the same in English, they have no connection whatsoever. In Spanish *a hangar* is **un hangar** but *a hanger* is **una percha**.

One of the most risky things you can do is to try and translate sentences word for word. This is particularly true of English phrasal verbs, which are made up of two parts: a verb followed by a preposition or adverb, such as:

> *ask in, ask out, ask around*
> *break down, break even, break in, break out, break up*
> *get about, get away, get by, get in, get off, get on, get over*
> *give away, give back, give in, give up*
> *go away, go for, go in, go off, go out*
> *hang around, hang on, hang out, hang up*

Each phrasal verb has to be treated as an item, not as two words. More often than not, the Spanish equivalent is a single word.

go 1 *vi* **ir**; 2 *vtr* ~ *after* **seguir, perseguir**; 3 *vtr* ~ *along with* **aceptar**; 4 *vi* ~ *amiss* **salir mal**; 5 *vi* ~ *away* **irse**; 6 *vi* ~ *back* **volver**; 7 ~ *before* **preceder**; 8 *vi* ~ *down* **bajar, disminuir**; 9 *vtr* ~ *for (choose)* **elegir**; 10 *vi* ~ *forward* **avanzar**; 11 *vi* ~ *out* **salir**; 12 *vi* ~ *off (explode)* **explotar**; *(leave)* **irse, marcharse**; *(spoil)* **pasarse**; *(alarm)* **sonar**.

look 1 *vi* **mirar**; 2 *vtr* ~ *at* **mirar, observar**; 3 *vtr* ~ *after* **cuidar, ocuparse de**; 4 *vtr* ~ *into* **investigar**; 5 ~ *for* **buscar**; 6 ~ *out* **estar atento**; 7 ~ *over (inspect)* **examinar**, *(overlook)* **mirar desde arriba**; 8 ~ *up (seek info)* **buscar**; *(contact)* **ponerse en contacto**.

break 1 *vtr* **romper, quebrar**: ~ *a record* **batir un récord**; 2 *vtr* ~ *away from* **separarse de**; 3 *vi* ~ *down (car)* **averiarse**; *(person)* **derrumbarse**; 4 *vtr* ~ *down* **analizar**; 5 *vi* ~*in* **forzar la entrada**; 6 *vtr* ~ *into* **asaltar**; 7 *vi* ~ *out (escape)* **fugarse**; 8 *vi* ~ *up (disintegrate)* **deshacerse**; *(relationship)* **separarse**; *(school)* **interrumpirse**.

If ever you're not sure which option to use, look it up in the other direction.

Never attempt a literal translation of idiomatic phrases, such as *the elephant in the room, to make a beeline for, to go cold turkey, pigs might fly.*

Spanish has lots of interesting idioms of its own:
pensar en las musarañas (lit. *to think about small rodents*) to daydream
aquí hay gato encerrado (lit. *there's a hidden cat here*) there's something going on here
abrir la caja de los truenos (lit. *to open a can of thunder*) to open a can of worms
irse de la olla (lit. *to leave the pot*) to lose the plot
tirar la casa por la ventana (lit. *to throw the house out of the window*) to spare no expense

ocho
needs must

Some verbs are more essential than others. If you were to analyse what you say in English over a day or two, you'd probably be amazed at how often the words *must, want, can, may, need, have to, should, could, might, ought* crop up. These are not words you can easily look up in a dictionary: in Spanish they're expressed by the key verbs **deber** and **tener que** *to have to,* **querer** *to want to,* **poder** *to be able to.*

You're likely to have come across parts of these verbs already, probably in practical situations:
¿Debo reservar con antelación? *Should I reserve beforehand?*
¿Tengo que cambiar de tren? *Do I have to change trains?*
Quisiera ver la habitación. *I'd like to see the room.*
¿Puedo dejar la maleta aquí? *Can I leave my case here?*
These verbs also play a vital part in general conversation: they allow you to explore possibilities and to voice your desires and your most mundane obligations.

They're easy to use and they all work in the same way, with the verb following them in the infinitive. Information can be tacked on to this: **Quisiera ver ...** *I'd like to see ...,* **Quisiera verte** *I'd like to see you;* **¿Puedes hacerlo?** *Can you do it?* **¿Podemos ofreceros una copa de vino?** *Can we offer you a glass of wine?* (See pages 162–163.)

what you have to do

There are quite subtle distinctions between the different ways of expressing need and obligation in Spanish. Although the English translations are similar, **tengo que** suggests a more pressing need than **debo**, the present tense of **deber**, while the conditional **debería** is the least urgent.

Tengo que saberlo. *I need to know*
Tengo que comprobar los detalles. *I have to check the details.*
Tienes que contestarme hoy. *You must answer me today.*
Tenemos que estar en el aeropuerto dos horas antes del vuelo. *We need to be in the airport two hours before the flight.*
¿Por qué tenéis que ir en coche? *Why do you have to go by car?*

Debo felicitarte. *I must congratulate you.*
¡No debo recordártelo! *I don't need to remind you!*
Debe saber si han llegado. *She has to know if they've arrived.*
Debemos despedirnos. *We have to say goodbye.*
¿A qué hora deben irse ustedes? *What time do you have to leave?*

Debería dejar un mensaje para Lola. *I should leave a message for Lola.*
Supongo que debería marcharme. *I suppose I ought to leave.*
Deberías comprobarlo. *You ought to check.*
Creo que deberíamos llamar a Pepe. *I think we ought to call Pepe.*
No deberían hacer eso. *They shouldn't do that.*

Irse and **marcharse** both mean *to leave, to go away*. The **-se** at the end of the infinitive in verbs like these changes depending on who the subject is: **debería marcharme** *I ought to leave*, **deberías marcharte** *you ought to leave*, **deberíamos marcharnos** *we ought to leave* (page 47).

Hay que is less personal than the above and often used for giving instructions.
Hay que tener cuidado. *I/We/You need to be careful.*
Hay que llegar temprano. *We/One should get there early.*
Hay que leer las instrucciones. *You/One must read the instructions.*

Deber + de can be used to suggest likelihood:
Debe de ser tarde. *It must be late.*
Su marido debe de tener cincuenta años. *Her husband must be fifty.*
Debes de estar cansado/a. *You must be tired.*
Ya debemos de estar cerca. *We must be close now.*

Had to is translated by the imperfect, the perfect and the preterite – but not indiscriminately.

The **imperfect** conveys *had to* in the sense of *used to have to, was/were supposed to.*
Todos los días tenía que esperar un siglo en la parada del autobús. *Every day I had to wait ages at the bus stop.*
¿No tenía que ir a menudo a Cuba? *Didn't you have to go to Cuba often?*
Teníamos que sacar al perro por las mañanas. *We had to/used to have to take the dog out in the mornings.*
Debía decir la verdad. *I/He/She was supposed to tell the truth.*
Debías llamarlo antes de llegar. *You were supposed/meant to call him before arriving.*
Debíamos ayudar a nuestra abuela cada domingo. *We were meant/ supposed to help our grandmother every Sunday.*
No debían llegar hoy. *They weren't supposed to arrive today.*

The **perfect** tense translates *had to* and *have had to.*
Miguel ha tenido que volver a la oficina. *Miguel has had to go back to the office.*
Hemos tenido que ir a pie. *We had to/were obliged to go on foot.*
¿Cuánto habéis tenido que pagar? *How much did you have to/have you had to pay?*
He debido comenzar de nuevo. *I (have) had to start again.*
¿Qué ha debido hacer? *What did you have to do?*

The **preterite** is used for single events.
Tuve que consultar el horario antes de reservar. *I had to check the timetable before booking.*
Tuvimos que que cancelar la cena. *We had to cancel the dinner.*
Tuve que irme enseguida. *I had to leave straightaway.*
Lucas tuvo que disculparse por llegar tarde. *Lucas had to say sorry for being late.*
Debimos aceptar su oferta. *We had to accept his offer.*
No debiste mentir. *You didn't have to lie.*

To explain what *should* or *ought to have been done*, you can use the conditional of **haber** + **debido**.
Habría debido comprobarlo. *I should have checked it.*
¿No habrías debido dejar un recado? *Shouldn't you have left a message?*
Habría debido ir con ellos. *You ought to have gone with them.*
No habríamos debido preguntar. *We ought not to have asked.*
Habrían debido sospechar algo. *They should have suspected something.*

what you want to do

Spanish has several ways of expressing what you and other people want to do. **Querer** is a key verb, and it's irregular in the **present** tense:

quiero, quieres, quiere, queremos, queréis, quieren

Quiero hacer una foto de grupo. *I want to take a group photo.*
Solo quiero añadir que ... *I just want to add that ...*
Matías quiere mostrarte esto. *Matías wants to show you this.*
Nunca queremos regresar. *We never want to go back.*
No quieren almorzar aquí en la terraza. *They don't want to have lunch here on the terrace.*

¿Quieres saber cómo funciona? *Do you want to know how it works?*
¿No quieres descansar un poco? *Don't you want to rest for a while?*
¿Adónde queréis ir después? *Where do you want to go afterwards?*
¿Queréis cenar o preferís picar algo? *Do you want to have dinner or do you prefer a snack?*

When talking about the past, English uses *wanted*, while Spanish uses the imperfect, the perfect and the preterite of **querer**.

The **imperfect** is the tense you'll need most of the time. It's about wanting to do something over an indeterminate period of time.
Quería mostrarte esto. *I wanted to show this to you.*
Quería saber si puedes quedar el viernes. *I wanted to know if you can make it on Friday.*
Cuando era pequeño, quería ser futbolista. *When I was a kid I wanted to be a footballer.*
Queríamos conocer la verdad. *We wanted to know the truth.*
No queríamos vivir en el extranjero. *We didn't want to live abroad.*
No querían ofender a nadie. *They didn't want to offend anybody.*

You use the **perfect** to say *have wanted to*:
Siempre ha querido ir a la ópera. *She's always wanted to go to the opera.*
Siempre hemos querido viajar. *We've always wanted to travel.*

... and the **preterite** when *wanted* refers to a specific occasion; often the outcome is known:
Quise comprobarlo enseguida. *I wanted to check it straightaway* (and I did).
Inma quiso darte la noticia. *Inma wanted to tell you the news* (and she did).
No quisimos despertarle. *We didn't want to wake him up* (and we didn't).

I want can sound rather blunt or demanding to English speakers, even though it is commonly used by Spaniards, so **quería**, which is the imperfect, or the conditional **querría** can be used to mean *I'd like*:

Quería **un kilo de patatas.** *I'd like a kilo of potatoes.*

Quería **saber a qué hora abre el museo.** *I'd like to know what time the museum opens.*

Querría **ver el puerto.** *I'd like to see the harbour.*

Querría **hacer un brindis.** *I'd like to propose a toast.*

Querría **verte otra vez.** *I'd like to see you again.*

An alternative to **quería** is **quisiera,** which is the imperfect subjunctive of **querer** and can have more of the idea of wishing about it.

Quisiera **un billete de ida y vuelta para Madrid.** *I'd like a return ticket to Madrid.*

Quisiera **reservar una mesa para esta noche.** *I'd like to book a table for tonight.*

Quisiera **verte de nuevo.** *I'd really like to see you again.*

Quisiera **ver la aurora boreal.** *I'd like to see/I wish I could see the Northern Lights.*

Quisiéramos **agradecerles toda su ayuda.** *We'd like to thank you for all your help.*

Querer isn't the only way of saying what you want to do in Spanish.

Desear *to wish, to desire*, is often used in formal circumstances:
¿Qué desean beber? *What would you like to drink?*

Tener ganas de has the sense of *to feel like, to fancy*:
Tengo ganas de ir a la playa. *I feel like going to the beach.*
No tengo muchas ganas de salir. *I don't much fancy going out.*
Los niños tienen ganas de ir al partido. *The children feel like going to the match.*

Apetece and gustaría (page 96) aren't only useful for invitations:
Me apetece explorar la ciudad. *I feel like exploring the city.*
Nos apetece comer un cocido madrileño auténtico. *We fancy eating an authentic Madrileñan stew.*
Me gustaría mudarme a un barrio céntrico. *I'd like to move to a neighbourhood in the city centre.*
Nos gustaría mucho verles. *We'd really like to see them.*
Me encantaría hacer un brindis. *I'd love to propose a toast.*

to-do lists

What you want to do and what you have to do are often very different things.

For the things you really have to get on with, you use **tengo que** or **debo**.

buscar mis zapatillas de deporte *look for my trainers*
comprar leche *buy some milk*
echar gasolina al coche *put petrol in the car*
cargar el móvil *charge my mobile*
sacar dinero del cajero *get some money from the cash machine*
ponerme en contacto con Rosa *get in touch with Rosa*
pagar la factura de la luz *pay the electricity bill*
mandar una tarjeta de cumpleaños a mi madre *send Mum a birthday card*
llamar a Tomás *phone Tomás*
decirle a Daniel que mañana hay partido *tell Daniel there's a match tomorrow*
(In Spanish you send to someone, phone to someone and tell to someone.)

Use **debería** for the things you ought to do but aren't urgent enough for the **debo/tengo que** list.

acabar el módulo/el proyecto *finish the module/ the project*
limpiar la casa *clean the house*
descongelar el congelador *defrost the freezer*
pedir cita en el dentista *make a dental appointment*
renovar el contrato/el seguro *renew the contract/ insurance*
cortarme el pelo *to have a haircut*
lavar el coche *to wash the car*
dormir más *sleep more*
ir al gimnasio tres veces a la semana *go to the gym three times a week*

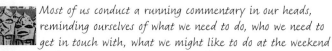
Most of us conduct a running commentary in our heads, reminding ourselves of what we need to do, who we need to get in touch with, what we might like to do at the weekend and so on. If you regularly use Spanish for this inner monologue, you'll find that it becomes a habit, one which results in a step-change in your progress. Try adding simple comments and questions: **How interesting, When's Will's birthday?, What a good idea.** It goes without saying that, whenever you're on your own, you can do this out loud.

... and wish lists

Querer is the verb for wishes and dreams, whether the decisive **quiero** *I want to* or the more aspirational **quisiera** *I'd love to*.

There may be things that you want to do in the short to medium term.
cambiar de trabajo *change jobs*
adelgazar diez kilos *lose ten kilos*
ponerme/estar en forma *get/keep fit*
hacer media maratón *run a half-marathon*
sacarme el carné de conducir *get a driving licence*
ir a Nueva York *visit/go to New York*
pasar un fin de semana en la isla de Menorca *spend a weekend in Menorca*

 List in Spanish five things you want to do in the next 12 months.

Think long term. Are any of the following on your *bucket list* **cosas que hacer antes de morir** *list of things to do before you die*?
nadar con delfines *swim with dolphins*
ir a Machu Picchu en Perú *visit Machu Picchu in Peru*
navegar por el cabo de Hornos *sail round Cape Horn*
ver el sol de medianoche en la Antártida *see the midnight sun in Antarctica*
ver el amanecer en el ecuador *watch the sun rise at the equator*
hacer un safari en Masai Mara *go on safari in the Masai Mara*
escalar el Kilimanjaro *climb Kilimanjaro*
vivir en el extranjero *live abroad*
bucear en la Gran Barrera de Coral de Australia *dive on the Great Barrier Reef*
hacer puenting *do a bunjee jump*

 Create **your** bucket list in Spanish, looking up any words you need, and say out loud what's on it.

what you can do

To say or ask what can be done, you use **poder**, which is irregular in the present tense:

puedo, puedes, puede, podemos, podéis, pueden

Puedo prestarte cincuenta euros. *I can lend you 50 euros.*
¡No puedo más! *I can't (take it) any more!*
¿Puedo verlo? *Can I see it? May I see it?*
¿Puedes avisarme si encuentras el sitio? *Can you let me know if you find the site?*
Podemos ir a tomar una copa juntos. *We can go for a drink together.*
Podéis aparcar enfrente. *You can park opposite.*
No pueden ignorar las dificultades. *They can't ignore the difficulties.*

Se puede *it's possible to, one can* is very common.
¿Se puede? *Can I? May I?*
¿Se puede pasar? *Can I get past?*
Siempre se puede coger/tomar un bus. *We can always catch a bus.*
Se puede aparcar en esta calle. *You can park/Parking is allowed in this street.*
Cuando se quiere, se puede. *When you want to, you can. Where there's a will, there's a way.*
No se puede tener todo. *You can't have your cake and eat it.*

The future of **poder** is also used:
No podré asistir mañana. *I will not be able to be there tomorrow.*
No podrán esperar mucho más. *They won't be able to wait for long.*

The more polite **¿podría?** *could I?* or **¿te importa si?** *do you mind if I?* are often used instead of **¿puedo?** *can I?*

¿Podría hablar contigo? *Could I speak to you?*
¿Podría proponer un brindis? *Might I suggest a toast?*
¿Quizás podríais acompañarnos? *Maybe you could come with us?*

¿Te importa si cierro la puerta? *Do you mind if I close the door?*
¿Le importa si nos sentamos aquí? *Do you mind if we sit here?*
¿Os importa si dejo aquí la maleta? *Do you mind if I put my case here?*

The English *could* has more than one meaning in Spanish. It can mean *would be able to* or *might*, in which case you use the conditional of **poder**.

No podría estar más contento/a. *I couldn't be happier.*
¿Me podrías ayudar a llevar las tumbonas? *Would you be able to help me carry the deckchairs?*
Podríamos invitar a los demás. *We would be able to invite the others.*
Podríamos cenar un poco antes. *We might have dinner a bit earlier.*

When *could* means **was able to/used to be able to**, you use the imperfect:
Podía ver el mar desde la terraza. *I could see the sea from the terrace.*
No podíamos esperar más. *We couldn't wait any longer.*
¿Podías oír la música? *Were you able to hear the music?*

The preterite also translates as *could*:
No pude hacerlo. *I couldn't do it.*
Pudimos abrir la puerta, pero no pudimos cerrarla. *We were able to open the door but we couldn't close it*
No pudieron convencer a los del otro partido. *They couldn't convince those from the other party.*

... while the perfect can express *have been able to* as well as *could*.
No he podido olvidarla. *I couldn't forget her.*
¿Has podido contactar con tu hermana? *Have you been able to contact your sister?*
No han podido completar la transacción. *They haven't been able to complete the transaction.*

There are times when *can/could* are **not** translated by **poder**.
When *can* means *manage to*, **lograr** or **conseguir** are often used, particularly in negative sentences:
No logro abrirlo. *I can't open it.*
No conseguí terminar el libro. *I couldn't finish the book.*
No hemos logrado encontrar la calle. *We couldn't/didn't manage to find the street.*

When *can* means *know how to*, **saber** (page 121) is used:
¿Saben nadar? *Can they swim?*
No importa si no sabes jugar. *It doesn't matter if you can't play.*
No sabía ni leer ni escribir. *She couldn't read or write.*

wordbank

Some of these commonly used Spanish verbs are regular, others irregular. However, when you're using them after **querer, poder, deber** this is not an issue — they simply slot in exactly as they are. They're arranged in pairs/groups to help you remember them by association.

aprender to learn
adivinar to guess
creer to believe
preguntar to ask, **pedir** to ask for
ofrecer to offer
aconsejar to advise
aceptar to accept
dejar to allow

enseñar to teach
saber to know (fact)
pensar to think
responder to answer
sugerir to suggest
ignorar to ignore
negar, rechazar to deny, to reject
prohibir to forbid

jugar to play
perder to lose
empatar to draw
comenzar, empezar to start

apoyar to support (team)
ganar to win
marcar to score
acabar, terminar to finish

mirar to look at
reír to laugh
escuchar to listen (to)
comprender to understand
mentir to lie
cuidar to look after
encontrarse con to meet

ver to see
sonreír to smile
oír to hear
aclarar to clarify
fingir to pretend
descuidar to neglect
evitar to avoid

abrir to open
tomar, coger to take
comprar to buy
gastar to spend
pagar to pay
poner to put
buscar to look for, search

cerrar to close
dejar to leave
vender to sell
cambiar to change
regatear to haggle, negotiate
quitar to remove
hallar to find

 Try learning these words in their pairs, by covering up first one and then the other. Then test yourself on the translations in a similar way.

 Deber means to owe as well as to have to.
¿Cuánto le debo? What do I owe you?
Me debe una disculpa. He owes me an apology.

knowing someone or something

Saber and **conocer** both mean *to know* but they're not interchangeable. **Saber** means to know a fact or to know how to do something; **conocer** means to know or get to know a person, to be familiar with a place or a concept.

saber: sé, sabes, sabe, sabemos, sabéis, saben
conocer: conozco, conoces, conoce, conocemos, conocéis, conocen

Sé que viven por aquí. Lo sé. *I know that they live round here. I know (it).*
Quiero saber por qué. *I want to know why.*
¿Sabes cocinar? *Can you cook?*
No sabe nada. *He knows nothing.*
¿Conoces el barrio? *Do you know the neighbourhood?*
Conozco bien Londres. *I know London well.*

Remember that when you use **conocer** with a person, you need a after it.
¿Sabes si Diego conoce a Isabella? *Do you know if Diego knows Isabella?*
Me gustaría conocer a Elena. *I'd like to get to know Elena.*

As you might expect, the imperfect translates *knew* or *used to know.*
No sabía si reír o llorar. *I didn't know whether to laugh or cry.*
¿Ya lo sabías? *You already knew?*
No sabíamos qué hacer. *We didn't know what to do.*
Cuando era estudiante, conocía bien Londres. *When I was a student I knew London well.*
Conocían todas sus canciones. *They used to know all his songs.*
No conocía el hotel; lo encontré por Internet. *I didn't know the hotel; I found it on the Internet.*

But in the perfect and the preterite, **saber** translates *learnt/heard/found out* while **conocer** translates *met/get to know*:
Ayer supe la verdad. *I learnt/found out the truth yesterday.*
¿Cómo supiste dónde encontrarme? *How did you know where to find me?*
Conocí a Esteban hace tres años. *I met Esteban three years ago.*
He conocido a mucha gente encantadora en la costa. *I have met a lot of charming people on the coast.*

> **Saber es poder** is a Spanish saying which means *To know is to be able to* i.e. *Knowledge is power.* Another common saying is **Querer es poder** *To want is to be able to* i.e. *Where there's a will there's a way.*

talking the talk

Lucía	Hola, no te he visto antes. ¿Es la primera vez que vienes a este gimnasio?
Rafael	Pues sí. Acabo de mudarme a este barrio. Antes vivía en Menorca.
Lucía	¡Ah! Yo nunca he estado en Menorca, pero tengo muchas ganas de ir.
Rafael	Menorca es muy bonita y turística, pero hay mucho desempleo. De mayo a septiembre es posible trabajar de camarero, pero como sabrás, en el sector turístico se gana poco. Tienes que trabajar muchas horas para poder pagar el alquiler y demás gastos.
Lucía	Ya me imagino. Mira, tengo que irme, pero quizás podríamos vernos otro día ...
Lucía	(*On phone*) Hola, Isabel. ¿Qué tal? Bueno, como sabes, la semana pasada conocí a un chico muy simpático en el gimnasio. Espero verlo hoy ... ¡No sé cómo se llama! Me tengo que ir. ¡Adiós!
Rafael	Hola, esperaba encontrarte de nuevo. Quería conocerte un poco más.
Lucía	Yo también. Si quieres, podemos ir a tomar algo.
Rafael	Me encantaría, pero hoy no puedo porque tengo que trabajar.
Lucía	No importa, pero quisiera verte otro día. ¿Dónde trabajas?
Rafael	En la clínica que está al lado del gimnasio.
Lucía	¡Ah! ¿Eres médico?
Rafael	¡No, qué va! Soy recepcionista y también me encargo de la página web. Me gustaría estudiar medicina, pero es una carrera muy larga.
Lucía	Sí, lo es ... hay que estudiar mucho. Pero, como dicen, querer es poder. ¡Tú puedes!

verb practice 5

1   Sort these into three groups under the headings **tener que/deber**, **querer** and **poder**:
    ought, could, was supposed to, wanted to, may, must, should have, would like to, can, had to, used to have to, used to be able to

2   From this chapter, choose ten examples that use the **yo** form of **deber**, **tener que**, **querer** or **poder**, and convert them to say *We ...* by changing the verb ending, e.g. **Quisiera ver el puerto** *I'd like to see the harbour* → **Quisiéramos ver el puerto** *We'd like to see the harbour*. Then change them (or different examples) to say *They ...* This will help you to remember the words as well as the verb endings.

3   Make sure you know the present tense of **deber**, **poder** and **querer**, then fill the gaps as quickly as you can — aim for less than two minutes.

a	deber	usted	vosotros/as ....
b	querer	nosotros/as ...	él/ella ....
c	deber	ellos/ellas	yo ....
d	poder	él/ella	yo ....
e	querer	tú	ellos/ellas ....
f	poder	vosotros/as	nosotros/as ....
g	deber	tú	nosotros/as ....
h	poder	él/ella	ellos/ellas ....
i	querer	yo	vosotros/as ....

4   Have a go at putting these verbs in the conditional, the imperfect and the preterite. Then use a few of them to create sentences, and say them out loud.

    The vocabulary in this and previous chapters will come in useful, but you might also like to personalise what you say by looking up some new words.

1   What's the difference between **Debo comenzar ahora** and **Debería comenzar ahora**?

2   Which is the odd one out from these expressions and why? **debí hacerlo, hubo que hacerlo, tuve que hacerlo, me apeteció hacerlo**

3   How would you explain that Luis has to leave and that he wants to take a group photo?

4   Arrange the following words to mean: *When I was younger I knew Edinburgh quite well:* **joven bastante Edimburgo cuando era más conocía bien**

5   How would you say *She must be fifty years old?*

6   Adapt **Tenemos ganas de visitar Barcelona** to ask a couple of friends if they fancy visiting Seville?

7   How would you ask someone (**usted**) if they mind if you close the door?

8   What's the Spanish for *I'd like to learn, I ought to learn, I must learn, I want to learn, I need to learn, I fancy learning?*

9   Using **querer**, how would you say in Spanish that *Adam would like to work in Spain but Julia doesn't want to live abroad* (**en el extranjero**)?

10 Complete this by putting **sé, sabes, conozco** and **conocimos** in the right places: ¿ .... **dónde vive el joven que** .... **ayer?** .... **que vive por aquí, pero no** .... **bien el barrio.**

11 What do the verbs **cambiar, vender, comprar, regatear** and **pagar** have in common?

12 A social media site has a **personas que quizá conozcas** feature. What do you think it's about?

13 The verbs *to read, to call, to manage to, to cry* and *to arrive* are all in this chapter and they all begin with the letter l. What are they in Spanish?

14 How would you explain in Spanish that you were meant to go on a cruise (**hacer un crucero**) last year but that you had to cancel the booking (**cancelar la reserva**)? Use *we* in your answer.

15 What's the Spanish for *I've always wanted to travel?*

nueve
sharing opinions

Whether you're chatting to someone you've met on holiday, socialising with Spanish business contacts, taking part in a cultural exchange or meeting your child's new Spanish mother-in-law, it's very satisfying to be able to exchange views on anything and everything.

Regardless of whether the subject under discussion is a mutual acquaintance, a local **cafetería**, the state of the beach, international sport or major issues such as climate change, terrorism or migration, the basic language structures you need are the same.

A point of view becomes much more convincing when it's supported. There are words that make an opinion sound persuasive and self-evident, such as **claramente** *clearly* and **obviamente** *obviously*, but what usually clinches an argument is a solid rationale and/or an impressive statistic or two.

As a foreign visitor, you might well be asked **¿Qué piensas de la situación política en tu país?** *What do you think about the political situation in your country?* Or, at least as likely, **¿De qué equipo eres?** *Which team do you support?*

asking someone's opinion

A useful way of asking someone's opinion of what you've said is to add *¿no te/le/os/les parece? don't you think?* Or you can use *¿Qué te/le/os/les pareció? What did you think?*

¿Es increíble, no te parece? ¡Qué voz tiene! *He's amazing, don't you think? What a voice he has!*
¿Es complicado, no le/les parece? *It's complicated, don't you think?*
Jugaron bien ayer. ¿Qué os pareció? *They played well yesterday. What did you think (of it)?*
¿Qué te pareció el debate sobre las elecciones? *What did you think of the debate on the elections?*

There are plenty of other options:
¿Cuál es tu/su opinión? *What do you think? What's your view?*
¿Qué te/le parece? *What do you think about it? What do you reckon?*
La situación es intolerable; ¿qué te parece? *The situation's intolerable; what do you think about it?*

según tú/usted/vosotros/as according to you/in your view
¿Según tú, es una buena idea? *Do you think it's a good idea?*
¿Según vosotros dos, cuál es la mejor solución? *What do you two think is the best solution?*

a tu/su juicio, a tu/su parecer in your view
¿A tu juicio, es suficientemente picante? *Do you think it's hot enough?*
¿A su parecer, es posible? *In your opinion, is it possible?*
¿A su juicio, ganará el nuevo partido? *In your view, will the new party win?*
¿A tu parecer, va a continuar el buen tiempo? *Do you think the nice weather will continue?*

Matters of current interest and topical concern are debated in Spanish **tertulias. Una tertulia** is a discussion circle or group that used to involve poets and literary types who would meet regularly in a café to talk about cultural matters. Nowadays it's a word which crops up all over the TV and radio schedules in the titles of discussion programmes. Topics are likely to include **el terrorismo, el cambio climático, el desempleo** and, of course, **el fútbol.**

saying what you think

The most straightforward way of giving your opinion is to use **a/según mi parecer** or simply **para mí** *in my view*.

A mi parecer, merece más de cuatro estrellas. *I think it deserves more than four stars.*
Son tan prácticos, según mi parecer. *I think they're so handy.*
Para mí, es una oportunidad que debemos aprovechar. *I believe it's an opportunity not to be missed.*

Another option is to tack **creo yo** or **pienso yo** to the end of a statement.
No es apto, creo yo. *I don't think it's suitable.*
No hay duda, pienso yo. *There's no doubt in my mind.*

You could also use **Creo que ...** *I believe that ...*, **Pienso que ...** *I think that ...* or **Diría que ...** *I'd say, I reckon that ...*
Creo que todos nacemos iguales. *I believe that we're all born equal.*
Pienso que los jefes ganan demasiado. *I think that bosses are paid too much.*
Yo diría que es serio. *It's serious, I'd say.*
Creemos que están todos locos. *We think that they're all mad.*
Piensan que el desempleo no disminuirá. *They think that unemployment will not go down.*
Yo diría que sí. *I reckon so. I'd say so.*

***

Creer **en** means *to believe in*:
Creo totalmente en el karma. *I believe strongly in karma.*
Creo sinceramente en la libertad de expresión. *I believe wholeheartedly in free speech.*
Yo creo en los extraterrestres. *I believe in extraterrestrials.*
No creo en el capitalismo. *I don't believe in capitalism.*

***

When verbs such as **pensar que** and **creer que** are used negatively, the following verb is in the subjunctive. (See next page.)
No pienso que ellos lo hayan hecho. *I don't believe that they did it.*
No creemos que todos sean terroristas. *We don't think that they're all terrorists.*
No creo que me ame/quiera. *I don't think she loves me any more.*
¿No piensa que su casa esté en esta calle? *Don't you think their house is in this street?*

using the subjunctive

The subjunctive isn't something you hear often in English, other than in expressions like *If only it were true ...* or *Is it essential that you be there?* In Spanish though, the subjunctive is used routinely, not only after **no creo que** *... I don't believe (that)* and **no pienso que** *... I don't think (that)*, but also when talking about wishes, opinions, attitudes — anything that isn't solid fact.

The **yo** form of the present tense holds the key to the subjunctive.
You remove the -o from **trabajo** and replace it with the subjunctive endings:

-ar verbs	-er verbs	-ir verbs
trabaje	coma	abra
trabajes	comas	abras
trabaje	coma	abra
trabajemos	comamos	abramos
trabajéis	comáis	abráis
trabajen	coman	abran

This formula works for the vast majority of verbs, e.g.
salir → yo salgo → salga etc.
tener → yo tengo → tenga etc.
volver → yo vuelvo → vuelva etc.

Just six commonly used verbs are irregular:

ir *to go* yo vaya	haber *to have* yo haya
dar *to give* yo dé	ser *to be* yo sea
estar *to be* yo esté	saber *to know* yo sepa

The subjunctive is very often introduced with **que**:
No creo que haya elecciones el año próximo. *I don't think there'll be an election next year.*
Es probable que vayamos a Madrid este verano. *We might go to Madrid this summer.*
Es imposible que ya sepa hablar a la edad de un año. *It's impossible that he/she can talk at the age of one.*
No es verdad que coma todos los días lo mismo. *It isn't true that he/she eats the same thing every day.*
Te recomiendo que des menos importancia a ese tipo de cosas. *I recommend you don't make an issue of those kinds of things.*
No pienso que Manuel todavía trabaje en ese banco. *I don't think that Manuel is still working in that bank.*
No pienso que sea gratis/gratuito. *I don't think it's free.*

Me temo que no tengan la menor idea. *I fear they haven't the slightest idea.*

Quiero que Pepe vuelva. *I want Pepe to come back.*

Espero que no llueva. *I hope it doesn't rain.*

Es preferible que vaya yo. *It's better that I should go.*

Dudo que Ana la haya visto. *I doubt whether Anna has seen her.*

Queremos que vengan a vernos. *We want you to come to see us.*

The subjunctive can be triggered by words such as **para que** *so that*, **a menos que/a no ser que** *unless*, **una vez que** *once* and **aunque** *although, even though*. Some trigger words are quite unexpected, such as **cuando** *when/once* if what follows has a future meaning.

Marcos nos esperará aunque lleguemos tarde. *Marcos will be waiting for us even though we'll be late.*

Se lo digo para que comprenda el contexto. *I'm telling you this so that you understand the background.*

Vendré yo a menos que llueva. *I'll come unless it's raining.*

Lo haré cuando pueda. *I'll do it when I can (i.e. when I will be able to).*

The subjunctive is often needed after superlatives too.

Es verdaderamente uno de los mejores helados que haya probado. *It's truly one of the best ice creams I've ever tasted.*

Es el peor hotel que puedas imaginar. *It's the worst hotel you can imagine.*

There's a lot to take in with the subjunctive. But you'll find that you soon start to recognise the endings when you hear them and they'll become increasingly familiar. If you forget to use them, don't worry: you'll still be understood. In the meantime, start getting used to them by choosing three triggers, e.g. **no creo que**, **espero que**, **para que**, and creating at least one short sentence with each.

When the verb before **que** is in the conditional or a past tense, you use the imperfect or the pluperfect subjunctive.

Me gustaría que Pepe volviese. *I'd like Pepe to come back.*

No pensaba que fuera gratis/gratuito. *I didn't think it was free.*

Dudaba que Ana la hubiera visto. *I doubted that Anna had seen her.*

Era la paella más sabrosa que jamás hubiéramos comido. *The paella was the tastiest we'd ever eaten.*

If you want to know more about these endings, see pages 167–169 and 174.

agreeing and disagreeing

The language you use to agree and disagree with someone has all to do with the context of the discussion. As in English, the expressions used in banter about football are different from those you hear in a formal political discussion.

agreeing

¡Genial! *Well said! Hear, hear!*
Desde luego. ¡Y que lo digas! *Indeed. Tell me about it!*
Es cierto. *It's true.*
Precisamente. *Precisely.* **¡Claro que sí!** *Of course!*
Tienes/Tiene razón. *You're right*
Estoy de acuerdo (contigo/con usted/con vosotros/as). *I agree (with you).*
Estoy conforme. *I agree.*
¡Exacto! *Exactly!*
Estamos totalmente de acuerdo. *We're completely agreed.*
Estamos en la misma onda. *We're on the same wavelength.*
Sin duda alguna. *Undoubtedly. Without the slightest doubt.*
¡Has dado en el clavo! *You've got it! You've hit the nail on the head!*

disagreeing

Lo siento, pero no estoy de acuerdo. *I'm sorry but I don't agree.*
No coincidimos en este aspecto. *We don't agree on this point.*
Ha habido un malentendido. *There's been a misunderstanding.*
No tienes razón. *That's not correct.*
Creo que te equivocas. *You're mistaken, in my view.*
Es cuestión de opinión. *It's a matter of opinion.*
¡En absoluto! *Nothing of the sort! Certainly not!*
¡Ni pensarlo! ¡Ni hablar! *No way! No chance!*
¿Estás de broma? *Are you kidding?*
¡Qué disparate! *Utter twaddle! What rubbish!*

> **bar-room debates**
> There are sayings that tend to crop up whenever there's a good argument.
> **En todas partes cuecen habas.** *Everywhere has the same problems.* lit. *They cook beans everywhere.*
> **Como en España, en ninguna parte.** *Typical Spain!*
> **No hay pan para tanto chorizo.** *There's not enough to satisfy all the thieves.* (**Un chorizo** is a slang term for *a thief*.)
> **Los políticos, todos son iguales.** *Politicians are all the same.*

making a case

A few useful phrases will help construct any argument.

en primer lugar *first of all*
en segundo lugar *secondly*
por un lado *on one hand;* **por otro lado** *on the other hand*
por mi parte, personalmente *for my part, personally*
en resumen *in short*
porque *because*
dado que, puesto que *given that, since, as*
total que *to sum up*
en fin *finally, to conclude*

Creo, por mi parte, que cobran un dineral porque **son personas verdaderamente talentosas.** *In my view, they earn loads because they're really talented.*
No creo que deban ser compensados, dado que **no han pagado impuestos.** *I don't think they should be rewarded as they haven't paid taxes.*
Quiero ir allí porque **he leído que es una auténtica maravilla.** *I want to go there because I've read that it's really wonderful.*
En resumen, **es un coche muy práctico y barato.** *In short, it's a car that's practical and cheap.*
Por un lado, **ella es muy inteligente;** por otro lado, **es algo egoísta.** *On the one hand, she's very intelligent; on the other hand, she's rather selfish.*
Dado que **son refugiados, deberíamos acogerles en la UE.** *As they're refugees, we should welcome them into the EU.*
Puesto que **no tenemos cifras precisas, es difícil hacer sugerencias concretas.** *As we don't have precise figures, it's hard to make concrete suggestions.*
Es aceptable, creo, puesto que **hay ventajas ecológicas.** *I believe it's acceptable as there are ecological advantages.*
Total, que **no pudimos salir del edificio.** *In short, we couldn't leave the building.*

> You can use **total que** where in English you might say *and so, all in all* or *to cut a long story short.* **Total** is also an adjective, as in **hay un caos total** *there's total chaos,* **en un silencio total** *in complete silence;* and it's a noun too: **el total** (or **el todo**) **es más que la suma de sus partes** *the whole is more than the sum of its parts.*

What do *you* think?

Yo diría que sí. Yo diría que no.
Estoy totalmente de acuerdo. No estoy de acuerdo.
¡Claro que sí! ¡Estás de broma!

Say each of the following statements out loud, and react to it
with a phrase from the box above. Choose a few of them and
see if you can add an observation or a further comment.
Consider recycling some of what you learnt in **Chapters** 4 and 6.

You can probably guess the new words but if you need to check, some
are in the wordbank opposite.

Los futbolistas ganan demasiado; los banqueros también.
Deberíamos legalizar las drogas.
Los beneficios de la exploración espacial son evidentes.
Tomar una copa de vino al día equivale a una hora de ejercicio.
El paracaidismo no es un deporte peligroso.
Tenemos la obligación de acoger refugiados en el Reino Unido.
Los políticos, todos son iguales.
El toreo es un espectáculo apasionante.
Es necesario erradicar los mosquitos.
El desempleo en la Unión Europea no disminuirá este año.
Todos nacemos iguales.
La violencia nunca será la solución.

Now express your opinion on at least six major issues by
mixing and matching these cues with some of the verbs and
the topics from the following wordbank.

A/Según mi parecer, … In my opinion …
    el gobierno debería … the government ought to …
    cada persona podría/debería … every individual could/should …
    los niños tienen que … children have to …

For instance:
A mi parecer, el gobierno debería concentrarse en la ley y el orden.
Según mi parecer, cada persona tiene que pagar impuestos.

afrontar *to tackle*

apoyar *to support*

aumentar *to increase*

ayudar *to help*

concentrarse en *to focus on*

contribuir a/con *to contribute to*

cuidar *to look after*

derrotar *to defeat*

desarrollar *to develop*

erradicar *to eradicate*

legalizar *to legalise*

mejorar *to improve*

mirar con lupa *to scrutinize*

pagar *to pay*

priorizar *to prioritise*

prohibir *to ban*

promover *to boost*

proteger *to protect*

reciclar *to recycle*

reducir/disminuir *to reduce*

respetar *to respect*

estar alerta *to be vigilant*

solidarizarse con *to show support for*

tomar medidas drásticas contra *to clamp down on*

votar *to vote*

ponerle fin a *to put a stop to*

la lucha por/contra *the fight for/against*

las medidas de seguridad *security measures*

la ley y el orden *law and order*

el extremismo *extremism*

la ciberdelincuencia *cybercrime*

el robo de identidad *identity theft*

las drogas *drugs*

el tráfico de drogas *drug trafficking*

la educación *education*

el medio ambiente *the environment*

las energías renovables *renewable energies*

el calentamiento global *global warming*

el cambio climático *climate change*

la exploración espacial *space exploration*

la economía *economy*

el presupuesto *budget*

los impuestos *taxes*

la evasión de impuestos *tax avoidance*

el salario mínimo *minimum wage*

los subsidios *benefits*

la austeridad *austerity*

los derechos humanos *human rights*

los derechos de los animales *animal rights*

la igualdad de oportunidades *equal opportunities*

la migración *migration*

legal *legal*, ilegal *illegal*

Build on three or four of your opinions. Try alternatives to gobierno and cada persona and expand on your views with porque or puesto que, for example: Es esencial proteger el medio ambiente porque el calentamiento global es un problema para todos, creo yo. Look up any words that aren't included here but that you feel strongly about.

using numbers and statistics in conversation

Statistics create the impression that you really know what you're talking about. If you need a reminder of Spanish numbers, go to pages 175–177.

Según las cifras más recientes, ... *According to the latest figures ...*
Las cifras/Los datos muestran que ... *The data/facts show that ...*
La realidad es que ... *The fact is that ...*
El hecho es que ... *It's a fact/a given that ...*

La realidad es que cuesta más de quinientos mil euros. *The fact is that it's costing more than 500,000 euros.*
El hecho es que el salario mínimo ha subido a quince euros a la hora. *It's a fact that the minimum wage has risen to 15 euros an hour.*
Las cifras muestran que menos de cincuenta personas se escaparon. *The figures show that fewer than 50 people escaped.*
Según el periódico, ganaron veinticinco millones de libras esterlinas. *According to the newspaper, they won 25 million pounds.*
En el estadio Camp Nou del FC Barcelona caben casi cien mil espectadores. *Barcelona FC's Nou Camp stadium can hold nearly 100,000 spectators.*

% is **por ciento** and percentages start with **el: el diez por ciento** *10%*; **el cincuenta por ciento** *50%*. A decimal point in Spanish is **una coma** *comma*: **diez coma cinco** *ten point five*. A point is used where English has a comma in numbers involving thousands and millions: **1.000.000**

Contiene menos del diez por ciento **de materia grasa.** *It contains less than 10% fat.*
Ofrece un descuento de hasta el veinte por ciento. *He's offering up to 20% discount.*
Los datos muestran una subida del cinco por ciento **respecto al 2015.** *The figures show an increase of 5% compared with 2015.*
Las cifras más recientes muestran una tasa de inflación anual del cero coma tres **por ciento.** *The latest figures show that annual inflation is 0.3%.*
Mira este anuncio de un piso en venta: cien metros cuadrados **y piden un millón.** *Look at this advert for a flat for sale: a hundred square metres and they're asking for one million.*
Todos nuestros productos son cien por cien **orgánicos.** *All our products are 100% organic.*

Alongside absolute numbers, Spanish has many words for approximate numbers.

Se ha ido a Málaga un par de meses. *He's gone to Málaga for a couple of months.*

Me quedo aquí unos diez días. *I'm staying here for ten days or so.*

He venido varias veces: quizás una docena de veces. *I've come here several times: maybe a dozen times.*

Nos vemos a eso de las cinco. *See you at about five o'clock.*

Esperamos cerca de tres horas. *We waited around three hours.*

Hemos visto cincuenta y tantos elefantes. *We saw 50-odd elephants.*

Gana quinientos euros a la semana, poco más o menos. *He earns more or less 500 euros a week.*

Ella recibió centenares de emails. *She received hundreds of emails.*

Han llegado millares de refugiados. *Thousands of refugees have arrived.*

Ordinals, i.e. *first, second, third,* etc. (page 177) are adjectives, so when they're used with a noun the endings have to agree.

Durante la Segunda Guerra Mundial ... *During the Second World War ...*

Es su tercera esposa. *She's his third wife.*

Leo es el quinto signo del zodiaco. *Leo is the fifth sign of the zodiac.*

Ana ha llegado al octavo mes de embarazo. *Anna's reached the eighth month of her pregnancy.*

Ha perdido las gafas por enésima vez. *He's lost his glasses for the umpteenth time.*

Beyond *10th,* you revert to cardinal numbers and these go **after** the noun, except when they refer to events, anniversaries and celebrations:

Pérez finalizó en la posición veinte. *Pérez finished in twentieth position.*

La bodas de plata se celebran cuando el matrimonio cumple veinticinco años; y las bodas de oro se celebran al año cincuenta de matrimonio. *A silver wedding is celebrated after twenty-five years of marriage; and a golden wedding is celebrated in the fiftieth year.*

Hoy se celebra el noventa aniversario de nuestro club. *Today is the ninetieth anniversary of our club.*

For monarchs, popes and centuries the same system applies, but both the ordinal and cardinal numbers appear after the noun. Numbers are always written in Roman numerals: **Felipe VI (sexto); Isabel I (primera) de Castilla; Juan XXIII (veintitrés); siglo I (primero) a. C.** *1st century BC;* **siglo XIX (diecinueve)** *19th century.*

more or less

To make comparisons in Spanish, you use **más** *more* + an adjective to express that something is *bigger, faster, more expensive.*

Los sueldos son más altos. *The salaries are higher.*
Este rompecabezas es más fácil. *This puzzle is easier.*
Laura es más joven **y** más guapa. *Laura's younger and prettier.*
Esta región es más interesante: **hay** más cosas que ver y hacer. *This region is more interesting: there's more to see and do.*

To say something is *the biggest, fastest, most expensive,* you simply add **el/la, los/las** in front of the noun + **más** + the adjective.
Es el centro comercial más grande <u>de</u> Europa. *It's the biggest shopping mall in Europe.*
La alerta terrorista se mantiene en el nivel más alto. *The terror alert is being kept at the highest level.*
Es una de las ciudades más baratas <u>de</u> España. *It's one of the cheapest cities in Spain.*
Son los hombres más ricos <u>del</u> país. *They're the richest men <u>in the</u> country.*

Menos means *less* and works in the same way.
Es mucho menos carismático <u>que</u> Pablo. *He's much less charismatic <u>than</u> Pablo.*
Este pueblo es el menos poblado <u>de</u> toda la región. *This is the least populated village <u>in</u> the region.*

Cada vez (lit. *each time*) add depth to comparisons.
La situación se hace cada vez más complicada. *The situation's becoming more and more complicated.*
La solución es cada vez menos clara. *The solution is less and less clear.*

The Spanish for *better/best* and *worse/worst* don't use **más** and **menos**.

Este sitio es mejor; **de hecho es** el mejor. *This site is better; in fact, it's the best.*
Explica mejor **lo que se debe hacer.** *It explains better what to do.*
La previsión del tiempo para hoy es peor. *The weather forecast for today is worse.*
Esta es la peor **crisis de su historia.** *This crisis is the worst in its history.*
Esta mañana se siente peor. *He's feeling worse this morning.*

talking the talk

Isabel   ¿Qué tal el partido ayer por la tarde? ¿Cómo terminó?

Javier   Muy mal. Perdimos. Aunque Torres marcó un golazo para nuestro equipo, justo antes del descanso ellos empataron con un penalti. Luego marcaron de nuevo en el minuto noventa y tres. Así que perdimos dos a uno. ¡Qué desilusión! Los jugadores parecían muy cansados. Me parece que no se esfuerzan lo suficiente.

Isabel   Es escandaloso. Con todo lo que ganan a la semana. Los sueldos son absurdos, ¿no?

Javier   Tienes razón .... En fin, vamos a tomar un café.

Javier   ¿Has comido en el bar de tapas que han abierto en la calle Nueva?

Isabel   Sí, una amiga y yo cenamos allí el sábado pasado, después del concierto.

Javier   ¿Que os pareció?

Isabel   En realidad, no nos hizo mucha gracia. Pedimos pulpo y estaba durísimo, y las patatas bravas no picaban.

Javier   Estoy totalmente de acuerdo. Yo pedí calamares, y parecían chicle, además había muy pocos.

Isabel   Y no es barato, ¿verdad? Es mucho más caro que los demás bares del casco antiguo.

Javier   Mira. Según el periódico, los precios de las viviendas siguen creciendo. Ha habido una subida del seis coma nueve por ciento en los últimos tres meses.

Isabel   Es un escándalo; hace dos años que Ángel y Daniela quieren comprar un piso, pero los precios están demasiado altos.

Javier   Es cierto. Aquí, por ejemplo, hay un piso en Vallecas: setenta metros cuadrados, dos habitaciones, y piden más de doscientos mil euros. ¡Doscientos mil!

Isabel   ¡Estás de broma! Y Vallecas es uno de los barrios más baratos de Madrid. Tendré que vivir toda mi vida con mis padres.

1 If you hear **según usted** directed at you, what are you being asked for? What other two phrases can you think of with the same meaning?

2 Having started an explanation with **en primer lugar**, how would you introduce your next point? And how do you cut a long story short?

3 How would you express *Hear, hear* in Spanish and say you couldn't agree more with the speaker?

4 If *extremism* is **el extremismo**, can you work out how to say *terrorism, capitalism, socialism* and *optimism*?

5 How do you agree to disagree by saying you have conflicting views?

6 Name two ways in addition to **porque** of introducing an explanation to support your opinion.

7 What does **sea** mean in **¿Usted no piensa que sea una buena idea?**

8 Put the right word in the gaps below: **lleguen, haya, era, venga**

   a   **Puede que .... perdido mi número.**

   b   **No supongo que ellos .... con retraso.**

   c   **No creo que Pepe .... hoy.**

   d   **Pensaba que .... gratis.**

9 **Hubiera**, **he**, **haya**, **han**, **habido** and **hemos** all come from the same verb. What's the infinitive?

10 Which one of the following needs a subjunctive after it: **creo, creo que, creo en, no creo que**?

11 What's the odd word out and why?

   segundo, séptimo, quinientos, noveno, cuarto

12 **Esteban es más joven que Miguel y tiene dos años más que Óscar.** Who's the youngest of the three boys? What's *youngest* in Spanish?

13 You probably already know **fácil** and **difícil**, so how would you say *less and less difficult* and *easier and easier*.

14 Fill the gap to say *hundreds of bees*: **......... de abejas**.

15 How would you say these figures in English: **siete coma cinco por ciento** and **cero coma ocho por ciento**?

diez
inside information

There's no better way of finding out about a place than by talking to the locals. They're the ones with inside information about what's available, how to do something, where to find the best olive oil, the cheapest petrol or a replacement charger for your phone.

Tapping into this local knowledge involves asking questions. The language structures you need work in most contexts: you simply slot in the relevant vocabulary. Don't forget the strategies on pages 54–55 for making sure that people understand you and that you understand their replies.

An unusual verb ending is likely to be an imperative. If you've come across directions such as **Tome la primera a la izquierda** *Take the first on the left* or **Siga todo recto** *Carry straight on*, then you already have experience of the imperative. It's used to tell someone what to do and how to do it, whether it's medical advice, a recipe or instructions for using a washing machine.

The internet is another obvious source of information. To access it via your tablet or smartphone in Spain, you may need two essential questions **¿Tienen wifi aquí?** *Have you got Wi-Fi here?* and **¿Cuál es la contraseña?** *What is the password?* In Spanish, **wifi** is pronounced *wee-fee*.

what there is

Hay *there is, there are* is the most simple of Spanish words yet among the most versatile, whether for seeking information or providing it.

You can use **hay** with a noun or with **para** + an infinitive:
¿Hay mucho tráfico? *Is there a lot of traffic?*
¿Hay almendras al pimentón? *Are there any smoked paprika almonds?*
Hay mucho ruido. *There's a lot of noise.*
Hay mucha gente. *There are a lot of people.*
No hay prisa. *There's no rush.*
No hay más remedio. *There's no other way.*
¿Qué hay para comer? *What is there to eat?*
¡Siempre hay algo para comprar! *There's always something to buy!*

It's equally useful in other tenses.

Había mucha gente. *There were a lot of people.*
No había buses para transportarnos. *There were no buses to transport us.*
Antes había flores silvestres en todos los campos, ahora hay muy pocas.
There used to be wild flowers in all the fields, now there are very few.

> **¿Ha habido un incendio?** *Has there been a fire?*
> **Ha habido una tormenta.** *There's been a storm.*
> **¿Ha habido retrasos?** *Have there been delays?*
> **Ha habido tantos debates.** *There have been so many discussions.*

El año pasado hubo un incendio forestal. *Last year there was a forest fire.*
Hubo muchos casos de tuberculosis en los barrios humildes. *There were many cases of TB in the poor neighbourhoods.*
¿Qué hubo? *How's it been?* (a Latin American greeting)

> **¿Habrá un baño?** *Will there be a toilet?*
> **No habrá problema.** *There will not be a problem.*
> **Habrá muchos espectáculos.** *There will be a lot of shows.*

¿Habría un riesgo? *Would there be a risk?*
¿Habría efectos secundarios? *Would there be side effects?*
No habría espacio suficiente. *There would not be enough room.*

... and what's missing

There isn't and *there aren't* are both **no hay**.
No hay tiempo/tráfico. *There's no time/traffic.*
No hay nadie en el auditorio. *There's no one in the auditorium.*
¿No hay mesas libres? *Aren't there any tables free?*

You can also use **faltar** to say that there's something missing or lacking.
Falta algo; falta alguien. *Something's missing; someone's missing.*
Falta el aire acondicionado. *There's no air conditioning.*
Falta Jorge. *Jorge's not here.*
Todo está perfecto. No falta nada. *Everything's perfect. There's nothing missing.*
Faltan dos vasos. *We're two glasses short.*
Faltaban los documentos más importantes. *The most important documents were missing*

Me falta works in a similar way to **me gusta(n)** *I like* (page 82).
Me falta un zapato. *I'm missing one shoe* lit. *One shoe is missing to me.*
Le falta el dinero para viajar. *He lacks the money to travel.*
Nos faltan las palabras para darle las gracias. *We don't have the words to thank you.*
¿Te falta algo? ¿Le falta algo? ¿Os/Les falta algo? *Is anything missing? Do you need anything?*

To say you're missing someone or something emotionally you need **extrañar**:
Extraño a Sofía. *I miss Sofía.*
Te extraño tanto. *I miss you so much.*
Extraño algunos productos típicos españoles, como los churros y los percebes. *I miss some of Spain's typical products, like churros and goose barnacles.*

... or **echar de menos**, which has the same meaning:
Echo de menos a Sofía. *I miss Sofía.*
Te echo de menos. *I miss you.*
¿Echas de menos Galicia? *Do you miss Galicia?*

getting advice and information

You can make a question such as **¿dónde está?** sound less abrupt simply by starting it with ¿me puedes/puede decir?

¿Me puede decir ... *Can you tell me ...*

> ... **cuál es la mejor marisquería?** *... which is the best seafood bar?*
> ... **a qué hora abre?** *... what time it opens?*
> ... **por qué falta Jorge?** *... why Jorge isn't here?*

> ... **dónde puedo encontrar la gasolina más barata?** *... where to get the cheapest fuel?*
> ... **dónde está la zona wifi más cercana?** *... where the nearest hotspot is?*

> ... **cómo funciona esto?** *... how this works?*
> ... **cómo se llega al estadio?** *... how you get to the stadium?*
> ... **cómo van?** *... what the score is?*

> ... **cuántas veces ha fallado?** *how many times he's missed?*
> ... **si está lejos el hospital?** *if the hospital is far away?*

You need si *if, whether* in questions without a question word.
¿Me puede decir ... *Can you tell me ...*

> ... **si hay agua caliente?** *... if there's hot water?*
> ... **si ha habido un error?** *... whether there's been a mistake?*
> ... **si tienes alguna noticia?** *... if you have any news?*

... and **lo** before **que** to mean *what*.
¿Me puede decir lo que ha pasado? *Can you tell me* what *happened?*
¿Me puede decir lo que quieren? *Can you tell me* what *they want?*

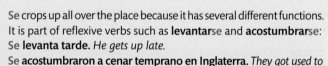

Se crops up all over the place because it has several different functions. It is part of reflexive verbs such as **levantarse** and **acostumbrarse**:
Se levanta tarde. *He gets up late.*
Se acostumbraron a cenar temprano en Inglaterra. *They got used to dining early in England.*

It can have a passive meaning, as in **Las casas se venden muy caras** *The houses are being sold for very high prices.*

It even has a role as substitute for the word **le** to avoid having **le** and **lo** together. **Se lo dije tres veces.** *I told him three times.* (See page 163.)

Se is also widely used like the English impersonal *one* in questions such as **¿Se puede comenzar?** *Can one/we/I begin?*

To ask *How do I ...? How do you ...? How does one ...?* you can use **cómo se** + the third person of a verb, i.e. the one used with **él/ella**.

> **¿Cómo se dice en español ...?** *How do you say ... in Spanish?*
> **¿Cómo se pronuncia esta palabra?** *How is this word pronounced?*
> **¿Cómo se sale de aquí?** *How do you get out of here?*
> **¿Cómo se enciende el televisor?** *How do we switch on the TV?*
> **¿Cómo se cambia la pila/la batería?** *How do I change the battery?*
> **¿Cómo se pone una denuncia?** *How do you make a formal complaint?*
> **¿Cómo se carga esto?** *How do I charge this?*

When the verb refers directly to something plural, it has a plural ending:

> **¿Cómo se abre este chisme?** *How do you open this gadget?*
> **¿Cómo se abren las ostras?** *How do you open oysters?*
> **¿Cómo se come un percebe?** *How do you eat a goose barnacle?*
> **¿Cómo se comen los percebes?** *How do you eat goose barnacles?*

¿Cómo se hace para + an infinitive is the equivalent of **¿Cómo se ...** and tends to be used more widely in Latin America.

¿Cómo se hace para encender/apagar el ordenador? *How do you turn the computer on/off?*
¿Cómo se hace para reservar online? *How do you go about booking online?*
¿Cómo se hace para conectarse a la red wifi? *How do you connect to the Wi-Fi (network)?*

 See how many similar questions you can come up with in just ten minutes. Use a mix of the words in the examples, some of the following words and any other words you know. Don't forget to say the questions out loud.

crear to create, curar to cure, encontrar to find (out), esconder to hide, evitar to avoid, garantizar to guarantee, hacer to make, to do, jugar a to play, llegar a to get to, preparar to prepare, recordar to remember usar to use

el ajedrez chess, el ataque de hipo hiccup attack, las berenjenas al horno baked aubergines, el cumpleaños birthday, el éxito success, el gazpacho chilled soup, la cafetera coffee maker, la luz light, el número number, la resaca hangover, la verdad truth

---

giving advice and instructions

Official signs telling you to do something use the infinitive:

TIRAR *PULL*, **JALAR** in Latin America
EMPUJAR *PUSH*
¡PELIGRO! NO ENTRAR *DANGER! DO NOT ENTER*
MANTENERSE A LA DERECHA *KEEP TO THE RIGHT*
APAGAR LAS LUCES *SWITCH OFF LIGHTS*
NO FUMAR *NO SMOKING*

When you're talking to someone, you use a less abrupt way of giving them advice or instructions: this is the imperative.

The imperative verb endings for **tú**:
-a for **-ar** verbs
-e for **-er** and **-ir** verbs

> **¡Espera!** *Wait!*
> **Firma aquí.** *Sign here.*
> **Come la corteza.** *Eat the rind.*
> **Une las dos partes.** *Join the two parts.*

You add **te** to a reflexive verb.
> **¡Cálmate!** *Calm down!*
> **¡Apresúrate!** *Hurry up!*
> **¡Levántate!** *Get up!*

The imperative endings for **vosotros/as** replace the **-r** of the infinitive with **-d**.

> **Llamad a los servicios de emergencia.** *Call the emergency services.*
> **Probad este postre: lo hice yo.** *Try this dessert: I made it myself.*
> **Tomad las pastillas con la comida.** *Take the pills with food.*

Reflexive verbs add **-os** in place of the **-d**:
> **¡Divertíos!** *Enjoy yourselves!*
> **¡Apresuraos!/¡Daos prisa!** *Hurry up!*
> **Acordaos de este número**. *Remember this number.*
> **Sentaos**. *Sit down.*
> **¡Callaos!** *Be quiet!*
... although **Idos** *Go away* retains the **d**.

Usted has its own imperative endings and adds **se** in the case of reflexive verbs:
-e for **-ar** verbs
-a for **-er** and **-ir** verbs

Tome una dosis cada tres horas. *Take one dose every three hours.*
Aprenda este número. *Learn this number.*
Abra esta lata, por favor. *Open this can, please.*
Aprovéchese. *Make the most of it. Enjoy it.*

Ustedes imperatives add **-n** to the above.
Tomen una dosis, Aprendan este número, Abran esta lata, Aprovéchense.

Predictably, the most commonly used verbs have irregular imperatives:

	tú	usted	vosotros/as	
ir	ve	vaya	id	*go*
decir	di	diga	decid	*tell*
ser	sé	sea	sed	*be*
hacer	haz	haga	haced	*do, make*
poner	pon	ponga	poned	*put*
tener	ten	tenga	tened	*have*
salir	sal	salga	salid	*go out, leave*
venir	ven	venga	venid	*come*

¡Dígame! *Hello.* (on the phone) lit. *Tell me.*
¡Sea honesto! *Be honest!*
Vaya con Dios. *Goodbye.* lit. *Go with God.*

When advising people ***not*** to do something, you start with **no** and then use the present subjunctive (page 128).

No me molestes. *Don't disturb me.*
¡No esperes un milagro! *Don't expect a miracle!*
No bebas/beba alcohol mientras tomas/toma esta medicación.
Don't drink alcohol while taking this medication.
¡No te muevas! *Don't move!*
No te preocupes. No se preocupe. *Don't worry.*
No comáis en aquella cafetería. *Don't eat in that café.*
No os apresuréis; podéis quedaros. *Don't rush, you can stay.*

everyday instructions

Many everyday phrases tell you to do – or not to do – something.

¡Anímate! *Cheer up!*
¡Ten cuidado! *Do be careful!*
¡Cállate, silencio! *Be quiet!*
¡Adelante! lit. *Go forward*, means *After you!*
¡Venga! *Come on!* or *Get a move on!*
¡No hagas caso! *Take no notice!*
¡No te metas! *Mind your own business!*

Some **recipes** use the **tú** imperative, others use the infinitive, and some use **nosotros/as** *we*.

Pon aceite de oliva en una sartén a fuego medio. *Put olive oil in a pan on a medium heat.*

Calentar un poco de aceite en una sartén y dorar el ajo. *Heat a little oil in a pan and lightly brown the garlic.*

Lavamos los tomates, los secamos, los cortamos en rodajas, las colocamos sobre el jamón y las espolvoreamos con una pizca de sal.
(We) wash the tomatoes, dry them, cut them into slices, layer them over the ham and sprinkle them with a pinch of salt.

You'll also come across commands when using Spanish computer software, which favours **usted**, or Internet browsers, which usually use **tú**:

Abre/a *Open*	**Cierra/e** *Close*
Guarda/e *Save*	**Imprime/a** *Print*
Haz clic en ... *Click on ...*	**Comparte** *Share*

Several Spanish expressions beginning with **que**, which look like instructions, are used to wish someone well.

A phrase you're likely to hear at every meal is **¡Que aproveche!** which literally means *May you enjoy/May you make the most of your meal.*

Que + subjunctive can be used with other verbs as well.

¡Que te vaya todo bien! *May everything go well for you. Good luck!*
¡Que tengas un buen día! *(May you) have a good day!*
¡Que te mejores! *(May you) get well soon!*
¡Que lo pases bien! *(May you) have a good time!*
¡Que sueñes con los angelitos! *Sweet dreams! May you dream with the angels!*

wordbank

computer talk

IT is **TI: tecnología de la información**; *computer* is **el ordenador** in Spain, **la computadora** in Latin America.

el portátil *laptop*
la tableta *tablet*
el monitor *screen*
el teclado *keyboard*
la tecla *key*

el cursor *arrow/cursor*
el ratón *mouse*
la impresora *printer*
la memoria USB *memory stick*
el cargador *charger*

el documento *document*
el archivo *file*
la carpeta *folder*
la hoja de cálculo *spreadsheet*

la base de datos *database*
el nombre de usuario *user name*
la contraseña *password*
el icono *icon*

el correo electrónico *email*

la dirección de correo electrónico *email address*

la bandeja de entrada *inbox*
el archivo adjunto *attachment*

los mensajes no deseados *spam*
los elementos eliminados *trash*

el sitio web *website*
la página web *web page*
el URL *URL* (oo ehreh ehleh)
el navegador *browser*
el buscador *search engine*

el favorito *bookmark*
el enlace *link*
la apli(cación)/app *app*
la actualización *update*
la ayuda *help*

abrir/cerrar *to open/close*
actualizar *to update*
buscar *to search*
borrar *to delete*
subir *to upload*
colgarse *to crash, to freeze*
descargar *to download*

editar *to edit*
hacer clic *to click*
hacer copia de seguridad *to back up*
mandar, enviar *to send*
mirar el correo *to check e-mail*
navegar *to surf, to browse*
teclear *to key in*

 Create ten sentences in Spanish, combining the structures on pages 142–143 with the above verbs and nouns: e.g. How do I turn the printer on? How do I go about uploading this photo? How does this document open? Or use other verbs you know to say you'd like to check your email, you want/need/ought to send an attachment/update or edit a file/find a link. Try asking if there's a password and what it is.

el spanglish

Spanish has long absorbed English words such as **el fútbol, el córner, el marketing, el networking, el jazz, el look, cool**. The phenomenon is called **el spanglish**, and new technologies are resulting in an increase in the number of English words used.

Like other borrowed words, they're used according to the rules of Spanish grammar. Nouns have a gender:
el hardware, un blog, un bloguero/una bloguera *blogger*, **un vlog, un post** (also **una entrada**), **un tweet** (although **un tuit** is the official version), **un tuitero/una tuitera** *Twitter user*, **el hashtag**.

In colloquial language **-ar**, **-ear** or **-uear** is added to verbs to create infinitives:
clicar, googlear/guglear, linkear, tuitear, taggear/taguear, bloguear ... and even **updatear**.
The new verbs use the endings of regular **-ar** verbs and have a past participle ending in **-ado**:
He googleado su nombre. *I googled his name.*

To chat is **chatear** and *a chat* is usually known as **un chat**. But you can only use these words for internet chats. To chat in the sense of *to have a conversation* is **charlar** (**platicar** in Latin America), while *a chat* is **una charla** or **una plática**.

If using a Spanish computer, you will have to get used to the fact that **el teclado** is differently arranged, making touch-typing rather difficult. There are a few questions which you might well need to ask.
¿Dónde se encuentra la arroba en el teclado? *Where's the 'at' symbol on the keyboard?*
¿Dónde se encuentra la almohadilla? *Where's the hashtag?*
¿Cómo se escribe el símbolo del euro? *How do you write the euro sign?*
¿Que función tiene la tecla bloq despl? *What does the bloq despl key do?*

As well as **punto**, **arroba** and **almohadilla**, it's useful to know the following:

, coma	; punto y coma	: dos puntos
/ barra	\ barra inversa	* asterisco
- guión	_ guión bajo	*space* espacio

shortcuts

Shortcuts are now an online phenomenon in Spanish as they are in English, especially on social media sites and in chatrooms. New shortcuts are coined regularly.

As in English, the aim is to be brief, while still comprehensible. Here are some of the more common ones:

toy **estoy**
bss **besos** *kisses*
kdd **quedada/encuentro/reunión** *gathering*
e-m **correo electrónico**
find **fin de semana** *weekend*
tqm **te quiero mucho** *I love you very much*
krisa **qué risa** *how funny*
mñn **mañana**
nv **nos vemos**
qndo **cuando**
dnd **dónde**
t **te**

d+ **demás/además/demasiado** *the rest, also, too much*
=/ **igualmente** *same to you*
* **beso** *kiss*

x on its own is **por/para** (**para** is also xa):
xti **por ti**
xfavor **por favor**

q on its own is **que**:
pq or xq **porque**

Numbers are used to represent parts of words or expressions as in English *great > gr8*, for example.

In Spanish **2** is **dos**, giving:
d2 **dedos** *fingers*
salu2 **saludos** *greetings*

Twenty is **veinte**, so **20** is used for **vente** *come with us*

1 is used for *a*:
1kf? **tomar un café/verse un rato** *have a coffee/meet up for a while*
dm1tq **dame un toque/llámame por teléfono** *call me*

keeping in touch

At the end of a visit, talk usually turns to keeping in touch. The highlighted numbers below refer to chapter numbers, in case you need a reminder of the structures used.

¿Cuál es **tu dirección de correo electrónico?** *What's your email address?* 2
¿Tienes **WhatsApp?** *Are you on/Have you got WhatsApp?* 2
Deberíamos **seguir en contacto.** *We ought to keep in touch.* 8
¿Podemos **intercambiar nuestras direcciones?** *Can we exchange addresses?* 8
Podríamos **crear un grupo en Skype.** *We could set up a Skype group.* 8

Ha sido **un placer conocerte/le.** *It's been a pleasure meeting you.* 5
¿Ha subido **el vídeo de la cena?** *Did you upload the video of the dinner?* 5

Mándame **un sms o un correo electrónico.** *Send me a text or an email.* 10
Me gusta **muchísimo la foto de grupo.** ¿Podría **adjuntarla?** *I love the group photo. Could you attach it?* 6/8
Contáctame **con FaceTime, ¿de acuerdo?** *FaceTime me, OK?* 10
No se olvide de/No olvide ... *Don't forget to ...* 10
    ... **compartir las fotos en iCloud.** *... share the photos on iCloud.*
    ... **escribirme.** *... write to me.*

Te llamaré **el domingo.** *I'll call you on Sunday.* 7
Te buscaré **en Facebook.** *I'll find you on Facebook.* 7
Te mandaré **todos los detalles por sms.** *I'll text you all the details.* 7
Te echaré **de menos.** *I'll miss you.* **Os** echaré **de menos.** *I'll miss you all.* 10/7

If you're planning to phone someone, it's worth knowing the following:
Dígame. *Hello.* **¿De parte de quién?** *Who's calling?*
(De parte) de Elena. *Elena.*
Soy yo/Soy Javier. *It's me/It's Javier.*
¿Con quién hablo? *Who am I speaking to?*
¿Hablo con Isabel? *Is that Isabel? Am I speaking to Isabel?*
¿Tienes el número de Isabel? *Have you got Isabel's number?*
Se ha equivocado de número. *You've got the wrong number.*
¿Quieres/Quiere dejar un mensaje? *Please leave a message.*
And if you're on your mobile (**un móvil** in Spain, **un celular** in Latin America), you might also need these.
Se oye muy mal. *It's a bad line.*
No tengo mucha cobertura/batería. *I haven't got much signal/ battery.*

talking the talk

Isabel	Esta tarde, ¿te gustaría cenar con Lucía y Rafael?
Javier	¿Quién es Rafael?
Isabel	Un amigo que Lucía ha conocido en el gimnasio. Parece muy simpático. Es su cumpleaños.
Javier	Vale. ¿Adónde vamos?
Isabel	Mmm. ¿Cuál es la mejor marisquería por aquí?
Javier	En mi opinión, es La Cocina de Paco.
Isabel	Cuando yo fui allí, había mucha gente y había demasiado ruido.
Javier	Espera. Voy a buscarla. ¿Has visto mi tableta? ¡Ah!, ¡aquí está!¡Ah no!
Isabel	¿Qué pasa?
Javier	He cambiado la contraseña y no recuerdo la nueva. Espera ...
Isabel	Venga, yo voy a buscarla. ¿Por qué no vamos a La Bandera?
Javier	Perfecto. ¿Cómo se hace para reservar online?
Isabel	No te preocupes. Ya lo hago yo.
Javier	Tranquila. No hay prisa.
Isabel	He reservado para las nueve.
Rafael	Invito yo.
Javier	No, paguemos a medias.
Isabel	¿Os apetece una copa en el bar?
Javier	Buena idea. Ha sido una noche estupenda.
Isabel	La comida estaba buenísima. El postre — ¡qué rico!
Javier	... Qué lástima que debes regresar a Menorca, Rafael. Aunque parece muy interestante el trabajo en la clínica.
Isabel	¿Cuándo te vas?
Rafael	Desafortunadamente, dentro de dos semanas. Es una oportunidad profesional que no debo perder.

Isabel	Adiós, Rafael. Sabes, Lucía te echará de menos. No te olvides de compartir las fotos online.
Rafael	Adiós. Ha sido un placer conoceros.
Javier	Que te vaya bien.
Isabel	Buenas noches, Javier. Hasta mañana.
Javier	Buenas noches. ¡Qué sueñes con los angelitos!
Javier	Bueno Isabel, eso es todo. Hemos terminado.
Isabel	¿Hay planes para la semana próxima?
Javier	No sé, quizás. Podría ir a Medina de Rioseco para ver a mis padres y a mi hermana. Hace muchísimo tiempo que no los veo.
Isabel	Pues … bueno … Gracias por todo.
Javier	¡Qué dices! Gracias a ti … ¿Tienes mi número de teléfono, ¿verdad?
	Deberíamos también intercambiar nuestras direcciones de correo electrónico.
Isabel	Claro que sí. Aquí tienes la mía – Isabel …
Javier	No hay prisa. ¿Te apetece un café?
Isabel	¡Vamos!

checkpoint 10

Most of the vocabulary is from this chapter but some of the language structures assume knowledge from the rest of the book.

1   What's the Spanish for *Is there anything missing/Do you need anything?*

2   Where would you expect to find **una arroba**?

3   **¡Aprovéchese!** *Make the most of it!* How would you say this to someone you'd call **tú** and to two people you'd call **usted**?

4   How do you ask if there's Wi-Fi available and what the password is?

5   If you're told **Se ha equivocado de número**, what have you done?

6   What's the Spanish for *There are a lot of people, There will be a lot of people, There were a lot of people?*

7   What word is missing from this question? **¿Me puedes decir ....
    que ha pasado?**

8   Can you remember what these random words mean: **chisme,
    noticia, cobertura, archivo, dosis, ratón, percibe, luz** and **red**?

9   What single word is missing from **¿Cómo .... apaga el ordenador?**

10 Tell a friend to *Try these almonds* (using **probar**), *be careful* (**tener**);
    hurry up (**apresurarse**) and *not to worry* (**preocuparse**). Now, say the
    same things to two friends.

11 Put these words into the right order to say that you really miss your
    friend Sofía: **Sofía mi a de echo amiga mucho menos**

12 How do you tell someone not to forget to do something (**tú**, **usted**
    and **vosotros/as**)?

13 Combine words from this chapter with knowledge from previous
    chapters to say the Spanish for *I have lost my memory stick* and *We
    need to buy a charger.*

14 Change these infinitives to express a) *I will ...* **escribir, guglear**; b) *We
    have ...* **despedirse, apagar**; c) *They did ...* **buscar, encender**. What
    do they all mean?

15 *It's been a pleasure meeting you* – how do you say it in Spanish?

grammar terminology

Adjectives are words that describe nouns and pronouns: *good idea*, *strong red wine*, *my fault*, *She's tall*, *It was weird*. In Spanish, unlike English, they change according to what they're describing.

Adverbs add information to verbs, adjectives, other adverbs and whole sentences: *a very good idea*, *He's acting weirdly*, *Luckily he's not here*.

Agreement: A Spanish article or adjective has to agree with, i.e. match, the noun or pronoun it relates to, in terms of gender (masculine or feminine) and number (singular or plural).

Articles are **definite**: *the house*, *the houses*, or **indefinite**: *a house*, *an area*.

The **conditional** is the verb form used to say what would or could happen.

Consonants and vowels make up the alphabet: the vowels are **a, e, i, o, u**; the rest are consonants.

The **endings** of words are the final letter(s). In English, a verb ending in *-ed* tells you it happened in the past. In Spanish, endings are much more widespread, with nouns, adjectives and verbs relying on them to convey essential information.

Feminine: See Gender.

Gender: In Spanish, every noun is either masculine (**m**) or feminine (**f**). This is its gender, and you need to know a noun's gender because words used with it, such as articles and adjectives, have corresponding masculine and feminine forms in Spanish.

The **imperative** is the verb form used to give instructions or commands: *Wait for me*, *Don't say that*, *Take the first left*.

The **imperfect tense** of a verb is used to describe how things were and to talk about things that happened over a period of time or repeatedly.

Infinitive: Spanish verbs are listed in a dictionary in their infinitive form, ending in **-ar, -er** or **-ir**. The English equivalent uses *to*: **hablar** *to speak*, **comer** *to eat*, **abrir** *to open*.

An **intransitive** verb is one that does not have a direct object, e.g. *to arrive, to laugh, to die*.

Irregular nouns, verbs or adjectives don't behave in a predictable way like regular ones and have to be learnt separately.

Masculine: See Gender.

Negatives are words like *not, never, nothing, nobody* and *not ... ever, not ... anybody, not ... anything.*

Nouns are the words for living beings, things, places and abstract concepts: *father, analyst, Siân, giraffe, chair, village, Madrid, time, courage.*

Number refers to the difference between **singular** (one) and **plural** (more than one).

The **object** of a verb is at the receiving end. An object can be **direct**: *He sent an email;* or **indirect**, in which case it is often preceded by *to* or *for: He sent an email to his friend.*

Ordinal numbers are *first, second, third, fourth,* etc.

The **past participle** of a verb is used with *have* when talking about the past: *I have finished, He has eaten, They had gone.*

The **perfect tense** of a verb in Spanish is used to talk about the past; it is equivalent to the English *I worked* and *I have worked.*

The **person** of a verb indicates who or what is doing something:
1st person = the speaker: *I* (singular), *we* (plural)
2nd person = the person(s) being addressed: *you*
3rd person = who/what is being talked about: *he/she/it/they*

Personal pronouns are words like *I, you, we, she, her, them.*

The **pluperfect** tense translates *had done something.*

Plural means more than one.

Prepositions are words like *by, in, on, with, for, through, next to.*

The **present tense** of a verb is used to talk about things being done now: *I work, I'm working.*

Reflexive pronouns are me, te, se, nos, os, se used as an integral part of reflexive verbs.

Reflexive verbs in Spanish have -se at the end of the infinitive: **llamar**se *to be called.*

Regular nouns, adjectives, verbs etc. conform to a pattern and are entirely predictable.

Relative pronouns are words like *which, who, that,* used to join together parts of a sentence without repeating the noun.

Singular means one, while **plural** means more than one.

The **stem** of a Spanish verb is what's left when you remove the -**ar**, -**er** or -**ir** ending of the infinitive.

The **subject** of a sentence is whoever or whatever is carrying out the verb: *They have two children, Anna reads the paper, This house cost a lot of money, Peace is possible.*

Subject pronouns are *I, we, you, he, she, it, they*.

The **subjunctive** is a form of a verb that's rarely used in English, other than in phrases like *if I were you*, but is widely used in Spanish in defined grammatical circumstances.

Superlative is *the most ...* when comparing several things.

A **syllable** is a unit that contains a vowel and consists of a single sound: *can* has one syllable, *can·ter* has two, while *Can·ter·bu·ry* has four.

Tense refers to when the verb is happening: in the past, present or future. Tenses have names, e.g. present, perfect, imperfect.

A **transitive** verb has a direct object, e.g. *to catch ..., to make ..., to open ...,* whereas an **intransitive** verb does not, e.g. *to arrive, to laugh, to die*.

Verbs relate to doing and being and are identifiable in English because you can put *to* in front of them: *to live, to be, to speak, to play, to think, to have, to need*.

Vowels and consonants make up the alphabet: the vowels are a, e, i, o, u; the rest are consonants.

grammar summary

nouns

Every Spanish noun is either masculine (m) or feminine (f), this is its gender. Nouns ending in a vowel add -s for the plural, as in English.

el chico *boy*	**los chico**s *boys*	m
el coche *car*	**los coche**s *cars*	m
la chica *girl*	**las chica**s *girls*	f
la calle *street*	**las calle**s *streets*	f

Most nouns ending in a consonant add -es for the plural, and nouns with an accent on the penultimate vowel in the singular lose it.

el camió**n** *lorry*	**los cami**o**n**es *lorries*	m
la mujer *woman*	**las muje**res *women*	f

A few nouns whose singular ending is -z have a plural ending in -ces: **el tapiz** *tapestry*, **los tapices** *tapestries*.

- Most nouns that end in -o are masculine and those that end in -a feminine. There are a few exceptions, e.g. **la mano** *hand,* **la foto** *photo* are feminine, while **el día** *day* is masculine.

- Some nouns ending in -e or a consonant are masculine while others are feminine: **el coche** *car*, **el calor** *heat* (m); **la calle** *street*, **la flor** *flower* (f).

- Nouns ending -d or -ión are feminine: **la edad** *age*, **la juventud** *youth*, **la estación** *station*.

- Most nouns ending -ma or -ambre are masculine: **el problema** *problem*, **el clima** *climate*, **el hambre** *hunger*.

- Adopted foreign nouns are generally masculine: **el blog, el sms.**

- Many occupations and professions have masculine and feminine forms: **el/la abogado/a** *lawyer*, **el/la cocinero/a** *chef*.

> Most of the time you'll be understood if you use a wrong gender but a few nouns have different meanings depending on whether they're masculine or feminine, e.g. **el capital** *money,* **la capital** *capital city*; **el Papa** *the Pope*, **la papa** *potato*; **el cura** *the priest*, **la cura** *the cure*; **el cólera** *cholera*, **la cólera** *rage*.

articles

In Spanish, the words for *the*, *a* and *some* depend on whether the noun with them is masculine or feminine, singular or plural.

	the singular	*the* plural	*a/an*	*some*
m	el museo	los museos	un museo	unos museos
f	la galería	las galerías	una galería	unas galerías

To avoid two 'a' sounds next to each other, **el/un** is used before a feminine singular noun beginning with stressed **a**:
El agua está fría. *The water's cold.*
Es un área natural protegida. *It's a protected nature area.*

Spanish uses the definite article more than English. It's most noticeable when talking about likes and dislikes: **Me gustan las verduras.** *I like vegetables.*
No me gusta la fruta. *I don't like fruit.* It's used:
- when making any kind of generalisation:
  Evita las grasas. *Avoid fatty foods.*

- before titles, when you're talking about (but not to) a person:
  El señor Rodríguez no viene. *Mr Rodríguez isn't coming.*

- with institutions: **en el colegio** *at school*, **en el hospital** *in hospital*

- with abstract nouns: **la guerra y la paz** *war and peace*

- with languages: **El chino es difícil** *Chinese is difficult*, but not after **hablar** and **aprender**: **Hablo chino.** *I speak Chinese.*

When **a** and **de** are followed by **el** *the*, they combine with it to produce **al** and **del**: **Van al mercado** *They're going to the market*, **el perro del alcalde** *the mayor's dog.*

Spanish doesn't use the indefinite article:
- with nouns denoting occupation or religion: **Es profesor/Es profesora.** *He/She's a teacher.* **Soy musulmán/a.** *I'm a Muslim.*

- after **qué** in exclamations: **¡Qué casa más bonita!** *What a beautiful house!*

Unos/unas *some* are used only with plural nouns, and are included in Spanish even when they're omitted in English: **Quisiera unas naranjas y unos limones.** *I'd like some oranges and lemons.*

adjectives

In Spanish, an adjective agrees with the gender and number of what it describes. This does not mean that adjectives and vowels always end in the same vowel.

Adjectives ending in **-o** have four possible endings:

m	**el museo modern**o	**los museos modern**os
f	**la galería modern**a	**las galerías modern**as

Adjectives ending in **-e** or **-ista** have two possible endings:

m	**el campo grand**e	**los campos grand**es
f	**la plaza grand**e	**las plazas grand**es
m	**el plan real**ista	**los planes real**istas
f	**la idea real**ista	**las ideas real**istas

Some adjectives ending in a consonant have two possible endings, e.g. **azul/azul**es *blue*, **cortés/cortes**es *polite*, **fácil/facil**es *easy*, **feliz/felic**es, **gris/gris**es *grey*, **joven/jóven**es *young*, **popular/popular**es *grey*.

Others have four possible endings; these include adjectives ending in **-án**, **-ín**, **-ón**, most adjectives ending in **-or** and adjectives of nationality, e.g. **charlat**án *chatty* → **charlat**ana, **charlat**anes, **charlat**anas; **trabajad**or *hard-working* → **trabajad**ora, **trabajad**ores, **trabajad**oras; **español** *Spanish* / **español**a → **español**es, **español**as.
There are no accents in the feminine and plural versions.

When adjectives and nouns are next to each other:

- Adjectives generally go after the noun: **un reloj pequeño** *a small clock*, **el camino largo** *the long road/path*
  ... but they can come first for emphasis: **un pequeño reloj** *a (very) small clock*, **el largo camino** *the lengthy/(very) long road/path*.

- Nationalities always go after the noun: **el turista francés** *the French tourist*.

- When **bueno, malo** and **grande** go before a noun: **bueno** and **malo** shorten to **buen** and **mal** in the masculine: **el buen tiempo, el mal tiempo.** But they don't change in the feminine: **una buena experiencia, una mala experiencia. Grande** changes to **gran** before a noun: **un gran teatro, la Gran Bretaña.**

- In the plural, adjectives describing a combination of masculine and feminine nouns use the masculine form:
  El vino y la tarta son españoles. *The wine and the cake are Spanish.*
  Mi hermano y mi hermana son rubios. *My brother and sister are blonde.*

Because of the different position of adjectives, Spanish abbreviations can be the opposite of their English counterparts, e.g. the Spanish for the *EU* is **la UE: la Unión Europea**, *the UN* is **la ONU: la Organización de las Naciones Unidas**, sometimes written **NN. UU.**

possession

	singular	plural
my	**mi**	**mis**
your **tú**	**tu**	**tus**
his/her/its	**su**	**sus**
your **usted**	**su**	**sus**
your **ustedes**	**su**	**sus**
their	**su**	**sus**

Mi hijo *my son*, **mi hija** *my daughter*, **mis hijos** *my children*.

The words for *our* (**nosotros/as**) and *your* (**vosotros/as**) have masculine and feminine endings, which agree with what's owned, not with the owner.

| *our* | **nuestro/a** | **nuestros/as** |
| *your* | **vuestro/a** | **vuestros/as** |

nuestro coche *our car*, **nuestra dirección** *our address*, **vuestros amigos** *your friends*, **vuestras opiniones** *your opinions*

In cases where **su** would be ambiguous, you can use **de** to clarify the meaning: **el libro de él** *his book*, **el coche de ella** *her car*, **la casa de ustedes** *your house*.

this, that ...

este/esta *this*   **estos/estas** *these*
ese/esa *that*   **esos/esas** *those*

- They go before the noun and agree with it: **esta página** *this page*, **ese ordenador** *that computer*, **estos ordenadores** *these computers*, **esas páginas** *those pages*.

- On their own, without the noun they mean *this one/that one* or *these/those*: **Me gusta esta; no me gustan esos.** *I like this one; I don't like those.*

- **Aquel/aquella/aquellos/aquellas** also mean *that* or *those*, and are used to point out something more distant:
  No me gustan esas casas, pero aquellas son bonitas. *I don't like those houses, but the ones over there are nice.*

adverbs

Many adverbs are formed by adding **-mente** to a feminine singular adjective: **lenta** *slow*, **lentamente** *slowly*; **feliz** *happy*, **felizmente** *happily*.

You can also use **de forma/manera** + feminine adjective: **de forma discreta** *discreetly*.

Common adverbs include **muy** *very*, **un poco** *a bit*, **demasiado** *too*, **tan** *so*, **bastante** *rather*. The ending of an adverb never changes: **Su trabajo es demasiado peligroso.** *His job is too dangerous.* **La comida fue demasiado cara.** *The meal was too expensive.*

comparing

Adjectives and adverbs are compared by using **más** *more* and **menos** *less*: **más cómodo** *more comfortable*, **más fuerte** *stronger*, **menos rural** *less rural*, **menos rápido** *less quickly*.

Than is usually **que**: **El fútbol es más emocionante que el ajedrez.** *Football is more exciting than chess.*
However, you use **de** before numbers: **Pagué mas de cincuenta euros.** *I paid more than fifty euros.*

El/la + **más** or **menos** means *the most* or *the least*: **la más cómoda** *the most comfortable*, **el menos probable** *the least likely*.

prepositions

Some prepositions correspond to more than one English usage.

a	*at*	**a las dos de la tarde** *at two in the afternoon*
	in	**Llegaron a Londres.** *They arrived in London.*
	to	**Voy a Madrid.** *I'm going to Madrid.*
en	*at*	**Nos quedamos en casa.** *We're staying at home.*
	in	**Vive en las afueras.** *She lives in the suburbs.*
		Llegamos en una hora. *We're coming in an hour.*
	on	**Está en la mesa.** *It's on the table.*
	by	**Voy en bicicleta.** *I'm going by bike.*
de	*from*	**a dos minutos del centro** *two minutes from the centre*
	of	**una taza de café** *a cup of coffee*
	's	**el hermano de mi amiga** *my friend's brother*
	for (purpose)	**el campo de golf** *the golf course*

| **para** | *for* | **una carta para mí** *a letter for me* |
| | *in order to* | **He venido para hacerlo.** *I've come (in order) to do it.* |

por	*around*	**Está por aquí.** *It's around here.*
	per	**diez por ciento** *ten per cent*
	for	**Cambié el viaje a Berlín por unas vacaciones en Venecia.** *I exchanged the trip to Berlin for a holiday in Venice.*
	by	**Es mas rápido por la circunvalación.** *It's quicker by the ring road.*

After these prepositions *me* is **mí** and *you* is **ti**. **Con** *with* combines with **mí** *me* and **ti** *you* to form **conmigo** *with me*, **contigo** *with you*:
¿Vienes conmigo? *Are you coming with me?*

subject pronouns

singular	1	**yo** *I*
	2	**tú** *you*: someone you call by their first name
	3	**usted** *you*: someone you don't know well (see page 14)
		él/ella *he/she/it*

plural	1	**nosotros/as** *we* (m/f)
	2	**vosotros/as** *you* (m/f): more than one person
	3	**ellos/ellas** *they*
		ustedes *you*

Because the ending of the verb is generally enough to show who is doing something, subject pronouns are used much less than in English, usually only for emphasis, contrast or clarification of *you/he/she*.

object pronouns

Object pronouns (*me, us, you, him, her, it, them*) can be the direct object of a verb: *Jon saw her*; or the indirect object: *Jon spoke to her*.

direct	indirect
me *me*	**me** *to me*
te *you*	**te** *to you*
lo *him/it, you* (**usted**) m	**le** *to him/her/it, to you* (**usted**)
la *her/it, you* (**usted**) f	
nos *us*	**nos** *to us*
os *you*	**os** *to you*
los *them, you* (**ustedes**) m	**les** *to them, to you* (**ustedes**)
las *them, you* (**ustedes**) f	

Both sets of pronouns normally go in front of the verb: **La lavo a mano.** *I wash it* (**la camisa**) *by hand*. **Diego me ha escrito.** *Diego has written to me*.

But when there are two verbs, one of which is an infinitive, pronouns can either go before the first verb or be added on to the infinitive: **Quiero cambiarlo/Lo quiero cambiar** *I want to change it*; **No la puedo ver el lunes/ No puedo verla el lunes** *I can't see her/you* (**usted**) *on Monday*.

The same rule applies for the immediate future: **Voy a escribirle/Le voy a escribir** *I'm going to write to him*; and for the present continuous: **Estoy visitándola/La estoy visitando** *I'm visiting her*. (An accent is added to the verb if the addition of a pronoun would otherwise change the word stress).

When direct and indirect object pronouns are used together, as in *I gave it to her*, the Spanish order is indirect followed by direct: **Te lo diré** *I'll tell you* (lit. *I'll tell it to you*, **Voy a comprártela** *I'm going to buy it for you*. If the indirect pronoun is **le** or **les**, it becomes **se**: **Se lo explico.** *I'll explain it to you*. **Podemos dárselo.** *We can give it to you*.

With imperatives, pronouns are added to the end of positive commands but go in front of negative ones: **¡Dámelo!** *Give it to me!* **¡No me lo des!** *Don't give it to me!*

Gustar *to like*, literally *to be pleasing to*, is one of several verbs that are used only in the third person, and are preceded by an indirect object pronoun. If what you like is singular, you say **me gusta** (lit. *it is pleasing to me*) and if it's plural you say **me gustan** (lit. *they are pleasing to me*): **¿Te gusta esto?** *Do you like this?* (lit. *Is this pleasing to you?*).
Others include **interesar** *to interest*, **encantar** *to love* and **doler** *to hurt*, because their literal meanings are *to be of interest to, to be enchanting to* and *to do harm to*.
¿Te interesa la historia de la Alhambra? *Are you interested in the history of the Alhambra?*
Me duelen los pies. *My feet ache.*
Nos encantan las patatas con alioli. *We love potatoes with alioli.*

redoubling of the indirect object

With third person indirect object pronouns, the actual indirect object is often identified again elsewhere in the sentence, preceded by **a**. This avoids any potential ambiguity.
Le compré un balón de fútbol a mi hijo mayor. *I bought a football for my eldest son.*
Les escribimos un email a Manuel y Rocío. *We wrote an email to Manuel and Rocío.*
Se lo di a María. *I gave it to María.*

It happens with verbs such as **gustar**, **interesar**, **preocupar**.
A mi hijo mayor le encantan las verduras. *My eldest son loves vegetables.*
A mi hija pequeña no le gustan los frutos secos. *My youngest daughter doesn't like nuts.*

Redoubling also occurs with *I, we, you,* but only for emphasis.
A mí me encantan el café. <u>I</u> *love coffee.*
A ti no te gustan las telenovelas. <u>You</u> *don't like soap operas.*
A nosotros nos gusta viajar en tren. <u>We</u> *like travelling by train.*
A vosotras no os interesa el senderismo. <u>You</u> *are not interested in trekking.*

personal a

Most verbs take an extra **a** when the **direct object** is a specific person or a pet.

Vi una buena película anoche. *I saw a good film last night.*
Vi a tu gato ayer. *I saw your cat yesterday.*

Conozco bien Madrid. *I know Madrid well.*
Conozco a tu hermana. *I know your sister.*

In these cases, the person/pet is still a direct object and is replaced with the direct object pronouns **lo/la/los/las**.
La conozco. *I know her.*

lo

Lo has other meanings as well as *him* and *it* (m).
It crops up in many everyday expressions, e.g.
por lo general *usually, generally*
por lo menos *at least*
por lo tanto *therefore, accordingly*
por lo visto *apparently*
a lo mejor *maybe, perhaps*
a lo largo de *throughout*
a lo sumo *at the most*
a lo hecho, pecho *what's done is done*
sea lo que sea *whatever happens, be that as it may*

Lo que has the meaning of *which/that which*, generally translated in English as *which, what, that* or *and this*.
Lo que quiero es una disculpa. *What I want is an apology.*
Juan llega tarde, lo que es un problema. *Juan is running late, which is a problem.*

He perdido mi teléfono, lo que significa que no puedo llamar a mi jefe. *I've lost my phone, and this means I can't call my boss.*
Volverá antes de lo que crees. *He'll be back sooner than you think.*

English words ending in -ing

An English word ending in *-ing* is conveyed in various ways in Spanish. The Spanish present tense translates both *I'm doing something* and *I do something*.
Trabajo con Emilio. *I'm working with Emilio/I work with Emilio.*
Ahora vivo en Tarragona. *I'm living in Tarragona now.*
Sucede hoy. *It's happening today.* **Sucede a menudo.** *It happens often.*

To make the point that something's taking place at the very time of speaking, you use **estar** + a gerund, formed by replacing the infinitive ending of **-ar** verbs with **-ando** and **-er** and **-ir** verbs with **-iendo**.
Estoy trabajando con Emilio. *I'm working with Emilio (at the moment).*
¿Qué estás haciendo? *What are you doing (right now)?*
Estamos comiendo bocadillos. *We're eating rolls.*
¿En qué estabas pensando? *What were you thinking about?*
¡Silencio! Estoy escuchando. *Shush! I'm listening.*

When the English verb is being used as a noun, Spanish uses an infinitive.
Me gusta trabajar. *I like working.*
Correr es mi vida. *Running is my life.*
Me hace bien practicar yoga. *Doing yoga does me good.*

An English adjective ending in *-ing* originates from a verb. Similarly, you have some Spanish adjectives ending in **-ante** (from **-ar** verbs) or **-iente** (from **-er** and **-ir** verbs): **apasionar** *to inspire*: **apasionante** *inspiring, exciting*; **convencer** *to convince*: **convincente** *convincing*.

The radical changing rule (page 171) is applied to verbs such as **sonreír** and **seguir**.
Clara está siempre tranquila y sonriente. *Clara's always calm and smiling.*
En los días siguientes, las visitas guiadas no se efectuarán. *During the following days, guided tours won't take place.*

Don't assume you can adapt all verbs in this way — in many cases a different adjective is used.

verbs

English verbs rely on subject pronouns to show who's carrying out a verb, as well as words like *does, was, were, will* to show when it's being carried out. Spanish verbs carry all this information in the ending of the verb itself.

There are three groups of Spanish verbs, their infinitives ending in **-ar**, **-er** and **-ir**: **esper**ar *to wait*, **com**er *to eat*, **viv**ir *to live*. Removing **-ar**, **-er** and **-ir** leaves you with the stems **esper-**, **com-**, **viv-**. Other endings can be added to the stem to convey specific information: **esper**o *I wait*, **com**e *he/she/it eats*, **viv**en *they live*. Each of the three verb groups has sets of endings, which can be used for all regular verbs in that group.

There are endings for each of the following:

present tense *happens, is happening*

future tense *will happen*

conditional *would happen (if)*

imperfect tense *was happening, used to happen, happened repeatedly or regularly*

preterite tense *happened, did happen*

perfect tense *happened, has happened, did happen*

pluperfect tense *had happened*

subjunctive *happens, happened* Based on the speaker's feelings, opinions, tastes rather than solid fact.

imperative *Happen!* Commands, instructions and directions.

gerund *happening* Used after **estar** to indicate happening at the very time of speaking.

past participle *happened* After *had, have, will have, would have* in past tenses.

The next three pages set out these various endings for **regular** verbs in each of the three groups, i.e. those that follow the standard pattern. Pages 172–174 show how many widely used verbs deviate from these patterns: these are classed as **irregular**.

the pattern for regular verbs ending in **-ar**
infinitive: **esper**ar *to wait*

	present	future	conditional
yo	esper**o**	esperar**é**	esperar**ía**
tú	esper**as**	esperar**ás**	esperar**ías**
él/ella, usted	esper**a**	esperar**á**	esperar**ía**
nosotros/as	esper**amos**	esperar**emos**	esperar**íamos**
vosotros/as	esper**áis**	esperar**éis**	esperar**íais**
ellos/as, ustedes	esper**an**	esperar**án**	esperar**ían**

	imperfect	perfect	preterite
yo	esper**aba**	he esper**ado**	esper**é**
tú	esper**abas**	has esper**ado**	esper**aste**
él/ella, usted	esper**aba**	ha esper**ado**	esper**ó**
nosotros/as	esper**ábamos**	hemos esper**ado**	esper**amos**
vosotros/as	esper**abais**	habéis esper**ado**	esper**asteis**
ellos/as, ustedes	esper**aban**	han esper**ado**	esper**aron**

	present subjunctive	imperfect subjunctive
yo	esper**e**	esper**ara**/esper**ase**
tú	esper**es**	esper**aras**/esper**ases**
él/ella, usted	esper**e**	esper**ara**/esper**ase**
nosotros/as	esper**emos**	esper**áramos**/esper**ásemos**
vosotros/as	esper**éis**	esper**arais**/esper**aseis**
ellos/as, ustedes	esper**en**	esper**aran**/esper**asen**

past participle	esper**ado**
gerund	esper**ando**
imperatives	esper**a**, esper**e**, esper**emos**, esper**ad**, esper**en**

the pattern for regular verbs ending in -er
infinitive com**er** *to eat*

	present	future	conditional
yo	com**o**	comer**é**	comer**ía**
tú	com**es**	comer**ás**	comer**ías**
él/ella, usted	com**e**	comer**á**	comer**ía**
nosotros/as	com**emos**	comer**emos**	comer**íamos**
vosotros/as	com**éis**	comer**éis**	comer**íais**
ellos/as, ustedes	com**en**	comer**án**	comer**ían**

	imperfect	perfect	preterite
yo	com**ía**	**he** com**ido**	com**í**
tú	com**ías**	**has** com**ido**	com**iste**
él/ella, usted	com**ía**	**ha** com**ido**	com**ió**
nosotros/as	com**íamos**	**hemos** com**ido**	com**imos**
vosotros/as	com**íais**	**habéis** com**ido**	com**isteis**
ellos/as, ustedes	com**ían**	**han** com**ido**	com**ieron**

	present subjunctive	imperfect subjunctive
yo	com**a**	com**iera**/com**iese**
tú	com**as**	com**ieras**/com**ieses**
él/ella, usted	com**a**	com**iera**/com**iese**
nosotros/as	com**amos**	com**iéramos**/com**iésemos**
vosotros/as	com**áis**	com**ierais**/com**ieseis**
ellos/as, ustedes	com**an**	com**ieran**/com**iesen**

past participle	com**ido**
gerund	com**iendo**
imperatives	com**e**, com**a**, com**amos**, com**ed**, com**an**

the pattern for regular verbs ending in -ir
infinitive   viv**ir** *to eat*

	present	future	conditional
yo	vivo	viviré	viviría
tú	vives	vivirás	vivirías
él/ella, usted	vive	vivirá	viviría
nosotros/as	vivimos	viviremos	viviríamos
vosotros/as	vivís	viviréis	viviríais
ellos/as, ustedes	viven	vivirán	vivirían

	imperfect	perfect	preterite
yo	vivía	he vivido	viví
tú	vivías	has vivido	viviste
él/ella, usted	vivía	ha vivido	vivió
nosotros/as	vivíamos	hemos vivido	vivimos
vosotros/as	vivíais	habéis vivido	vivisteis
ellos/as, ustedes	vivían	han vivido	vivieron

	present subjunctive	imperfect subjunctive
yo	viva	viviera/viviese
tú	vivas	vivieras/vivieses
él/ella, usted	viva	viviera/viviese
nosotros/as	vivamos	viviéramos/viviésemos
vosotros/as	viváis	vivierais/vivieseis
ellos/as, ustedes	vivan	vivieran/viviesen

past participle   vivido
gerund   viviendo
imperatives   vive, viva, vivamos, vivid, vivan

reflexive verbs

The infinitive of reflexive verbs ends in **-se: llamarse** *to be called*, **levantarse** *to get up*, **casarse** *to get married*. These verbs follow exactly the same pattern of endings as regular -ar, -er, and -ir verbs but they include **me, te, se, nos, os** before the verb according to who/what is involved.

	present	perfect
yo	me **levanto**	me **he levantado**
tú	te **levantas**	te **has levantado**
él/ella, usted	se **levanta**	se **ha levantado**
nosotros/as	nos **levantamos**	nos **hemos levantado**
vosotros/as	os **levantáis**	os **habéis levantado**
ellos/as, ustedes	se **levantan**	se **han levantado**

questions

Spanish doesn't use extra words like *do, does* in a question; you raise the pitch of your voice at the end so that it *sounds* like a question.
Ana se va hoy. *Ana leaves/is leaving today.*
¿Ana se va hoy? *Is Ana leaving today?*
Llega con retraso. *It's arriving late.*
¿Llega con retraso? *Is it arriving late?*
Entienden. *They understand.*
¿Entienden? *Do they understand?*

negatives

Do, does are not used in negatives. To say something negative, you simply put **no** in front of the verb.
Trabajo en Barcelona. *I work/I'm working in Barcelona.*
No trabajo en Barcelona. *I don't work/I'm not working in Barcelona.*
Entienden. *They understand.*
No entienden. *They don't understand.*
Han entendido. *They have understood.*
¿No han entendido? *Haven't they understood?*

In Spanish, unlike English, both **no** and a negative word like **nada** *nothing* can be used in the same sentence.
No quiere nada. *He/She does not want anything.*
No hemos visto nada. *We've seen nothing.*
No queda nadie. *There's nobody left.*
No he ido nunca a Portugal. *I've never been to Portugal.*

radical changing verbs

There are several common verbs which use the regular present tense endings but which change the vowel **e** or **o** in their stem for all persons except **nosotros/as** and **vosotros/as**.

e → ie

querer to want	→	**quiero** I want, **queremos** we want
sentir to feel	→	**siente** she feels, **sienten** they feel
preferir to prefer	→	**prefiero** I prefer, **prefieres** you prefer (**tú**)

Others include **cerrar** to close, **comenzar** to start, **pensar** to think, **entender** to understand.

e → i occurs only in -**ir** verbs, such as **servir** to serve as well as:

pedir to ask for	→	**pido** I ask for, **pedimos** we ask for
seguir to follow	→	**sigues** you follow (**tú**), **seguís** you follow (**vosotros/as**)

o → ue

dormir to sleep	→	**duerme** he/she sleeps, **dormimos** we sleep
costar to cost	→	**cuesta** it costs, **cuestan** they cost

Others include **contar** to count, **encontrar** to find, **recordar** to remember, **poder** to be able to, **volver** to return.

The vowel also changes in **jugar** to play (u → ue): **juego** I play, **juegan** they play.

In the preterite, the -**ar** and -**er** verbs are regular, but the vowel in the stem of the -**ir** verbs changes in the *he/she* and *they* forms. The change is different from the one that occurs in the present tense:

dormir to sleep → **dormí** I slept, **durmió** he/she slept, **durmieron** they slept
preferir to prefer→ **preferí** I preferred, **prefirió** he/she preferred

irregular verbs

Some verbs deviate significantly from the regular patterns in one, some or all their tenses.

present tense

caer *to fall*: **caigo, caes, cae, caemos, caéis, caen**
dar *to give*: **doy, das, da, damos, dais, dan**
decir to say: **digo, dices, dice, decimos, decís, dicen**
estar *to be*: **estoy, estás, está, estamos, estáis, están**
haber *to have*: **he, has, ha, hemos, habéis, han**
hacer *to do, make*: **hago, haces, hace, hacemos, hacéis, hacen**
ir *to go*: **voy, vas, va, vamos, vais, van**
poder *to be able to*: **puedo, puedes, puede, podemos, podéis, pueden**
querer *to want*: **quiero, quieres, quiere, queremos, queréis, quieren**
saber *to know*: **sé, sabes, sabe, sabemos, sabéis, saben**
ser *to be*: **soy, eres, es, somos, sois, son**
tener *to have, to hold*: **tengo, tienes, tiene, tenemos, tenéis, tienen**
venir *to come*: **vengo, vienes, viene, venimos, venís, vienen**
volver *to return*: **vuelvo, vuelves, vuelve, volvemos, volvéis, vuelven**

imperfect tense

ir *to go*: **iba, ibas, iba, íbamos, ibais, iban**
ser *to be*: **era, eras, era, éramos, erais, eran**
ver to see: **veía, veías, veía, veíamos, veíais, veían**

preterite tense

andar *to walk*: **anduve, anduviste, anduvo, anduvimos, anduvisteis, anduvieron**
caer *to fall*: **caí, caiste, cayó, caimos, caísteis, cayeron**
conducir *to drive*: **conduje, condujiste, condujo, condujimos, condujisteis, condujeron**
dar *to give*: **di, diste, dio, dimos, disteis, dieron**
decir *to say*: **dije, dijiste, dijo, dijimos, dijisteis, dijeron**
estar *to be*: **estuve, estuviste, estuvo, estuvimos, estuvisteis, estuvieron**
hacer *to do, to make*: **hice, hiciste, hizo, hicimos, hicisteis, hicieron**
ir *to go*: **fui, fuiste, fue, fuimos, fuisteis, fueron**
poder *to be able*: **pude, pudiste, pudo, pudimos, pudisteis, pudieron**
poner *to put*: **puse, pusiste, puso, pusimos, pusisteis, pusieron**
querer *to want*: **quise, quisiste, quiso, quisimos, quisisteis, quisieron**
saber *to know*: **supe, supiste, supo, supimos, supisteis, supieron**

ser *to be*: **fui, fuiste, fue, fuimos, fuisteis, fueron**
tener *to have, to hold*: **tuve, tuviste, tuvo, tuvimos, tuvisteis, tuvieron**
traer *to bring*: **traje, trajiste, trajo, trajimos, trajisteis, trajeron**
venir *to come*: **vine, viniste, vino, vinimos, vinisteis, vinieron**
ver *to see*: **vi, viste, vio, vimos, visteis, vieron**

future tense

caber *to fit*: **cabré, cabrás, cabrá, cabremos, cabréis, cabrán**
decir *to say*: **diré, dirás, dirá, diremos, diréis, dirán**
haber *to have*: **habré, habrás, habrá, habremos, habréis, habrán**
hacer *to do, to make*: **haré, harás, hará, haremos, haréis, harán**
poder *to be able*: **podré, podrás, podrá, podremos, podréis, podrán**
poner *to put*: **pondré, pondrás, pondrá, pondremos, pondréis, pondrán**
querer *to want*: **querré, querrás, querrá, querremos, querréis, querrán**
saber *to know*: **sabré, sabrás, sabrá, sabremos, sabréis, sabrán**
salir *to leave*: **saldré, saldrás, saldrá, saldremos, saldréis, saldrán**
tener *to have, to hold*: **tendré, tendrás, tendrá, tendremos, tendréis, tendrán**
valer *to be worth*: **valdré, valdrás, valdrá, valdremos, valdréis, valdrán**
venir *to come*: **vendré, vendrás, vendrá, vendremos, vendréis, vendrán**

conditional

Regular conditional endings are added to the future stem, e.g:
hacer *to do, to make*: **haría, harías, haría, haríamos, haríais, harían**
querer *to want*: **querría, querrías, querría, querríamos, querríais, querrían**

present subjunctive

dar *to give*: **dé, des, dé, demos, deis, den**
decir *to say*: **diga, digas, diga, digamos, digáis, digan**
estar *to be*: **esté, estés, esté, estemos, estéis, estén**
haber *to have*: **haya, hayas, haya, hayamos hayáis, hayan**
hacer *to do, to make*: **haga, hagas, haga, hagamos,hagáis, hagan**
ir *to go*: **vaya, vayas, vaya, vayamos, vayáis, vayan**
poder *to be able to*: **pueda, puedas, pueda, podamos, podáis, puedan**
querer *to want*: **quiera, quieras, quiera, queramos, queráis, quieran**
saber *to know*: **sepa, sepas, sepa, sepamos, sepáis, sepan**
ser *to be*: **sea, seas, sea, seamos, seáis, sean**
tener *to have, to hold*: **tenga, tengas, tenga, tengamos, tengáis, tengan**
venir *to come*: **venga, vengas, venga, vengamos, vengáis, vengan**
volver *to return*: **vuelva, vuelvas, vuelva, volvamos, volváis, vuelvan**

imperfect subjunctive

Verbs which are irregular in the preterite (above) have similarly irregular subjunctives. The basis, called the stem, is the third person plural of the preterite: **fueron, dieron** etc. Take off the **-ron** and replace it with the imperfect subjunctive endings. Here are some examples:

ser *to be* and **ir** *to go*: **fuera, fueras, fuera, fuéramos, fuerais, fueran**

decir *to say*: **dijera, dijeras, dijera, dijéramos, dijerais, dijeran**

tener *to have, to hold*: **tuviera, tuvieras, tuviera, tuviéramos, tuvierais, tuvieran**

In the **nosotros/as** form you add an accent on the first **-e**.

There is also a set of less commonly used alternative endings that you may come across: **fuese, fueses, fuese, fuésemos, fueseis, fuesen**

dijese, dijeses, dijese, dijésemos, dijeseis, dijesen

tuviese, tuvieses, tuviese, tuviésemos, tuvieseis, tuviesen

imperative

infinitive	tú	usted	vosotros/as
decir *to say*	**di**	**diga**	**decid**
hacer *to do, to make*	**haz**	**haga**	**haced**
ir *to go*	**ve**	**vaya**	**id**
poner *to put*	**pon**	**ponga**	**poned**
salir *to leave*	**sal**	**salga**	**salid**
ser *to be*	**sé**	**sea**	**sed**
tener *to have, to hold*	**ten**	**tenga**	**tened**
venir *to come*	**ven**	**venga**	**venid**

past participle

abrir *to open*: **abierto**

cubrir *to cover*: **cubierto**

decir *to say*: **dicho**

descubrir *to discover*: **descubierto**

escribir *to write*: **escrito**

hacer *to do, to make*: **hecho**

morir *to die*: **muerto**

poner *to put*: **puesto**

romper *to break*: **roto**

ver *to see*: **visto**

volver *to return*: **vuelto**

numbers

numbers 1–99

0	cero		
1	uno	11	once
2	dos	12	doce
3	tres	13	trece
4	cuatro	14	catorce
5	cinco	15	quince
6	seis	16	dieciséis
7	siete	17	diecisiete
8	ocho	18	dieciocho
9	nueve	19	diecinueve
10	diez	20	veinte

21	veintiuno	31	treinta y uno
22	veintidós	32	treinta y dos
23	veintitrés	33	treinta y tres
24	veinticuatro	34	treinta y cuatro
25	veinticinco	35	treinta y cinco
26	veintiséis	36	treinta y seis
27	veintisiete	37	treinta y siete
28	veintiocho	38	treinta y ocho
29	veintinueve	39	treinta y nueve
30	treinta	40	cuarenta

50	cincuenta
60	sesenta
70	setenta
80	ochenta
90	noventa

41–99 follow the same pattern as 31–19:
cuarenta y uno … noventa y nueve

- **Cero** translates *zero, nought, nil, love* (tennis) and *O* (telephone). The plural is **ceros: dos ceros** *two noughts.*

- **Uno** and numbers ending in uno, such as **veintiuno** and **treinta y uno**, change to agree with the noun, dropping the **-o** before masculine nouns, gaining an **-a** before feminine ones: **un adulto; una persona**

numbers 100 +

100	cien
101	ciento uno
102	ciento dos
110	ciento diez
120	ciento veinte
125	ciento veinticinco
150	ciento cincuenta
155	ciento cincuenta y cinco
199	ciento noventa y nueve
200	doscientos
250	doscientos cincuenta
300	trescientos
500	quinientos
700	setecientos
900	novecientos
999	novecientos noventa y nueve
1 000	mil
1 100	mil cien
1 500	mil quinientos
2 000	dos mil
10 000	diez mil
100 000	cien mil
500 000	quinientos mil
1 000 000	un millón
2 000 000	dos millones

Cien *100*, a shortened form of **ciento**, never has **un** in front of it. It's used on its own and in front of a noun: **cien veces** *a hundred times*, **cien metros** *100 metres*. It's also used in front of a number larger than 100: **cien billones** *a hundred billion*, but **ciento** is used before a number smaller than 100: **ciento cincuenta** *a hundred and fifty*.

The plural has a masculine and a feminine version: **trescientos grados** *300 degrees*, **quinientas personas** *500 people*.

Spanish uses a comma where the UK has a decimal point:

10,5: diez coma cinco *10.5: ten point five.*

Las cifras muestran una tasa de inflación del cero coma tres por ciento. *The figures show a rate of inflation of 0.3%.*

first, second, third, etc.

1st	**1°**	**primero**
2nd	**2°**	**segundo**
3rd	**3°**	**tercero**
4th	**4°**	**cuarto**
5th	**5°**	**quinto**
6th	**6°**	**sexto**
7th	**7°**	**séptimo**
8th	**8°**	**octavo**
9th	**9°**	**noveno**
10th	**10°**	**décimo**

The endings of these numbers used with a noun have to agree because they're adjectives:

la primera vez *first time*
los segundos platos *second (main) courses*
la tercera edad *the third age*
el quinto elemento *the fifth element*

Primero and **tercero** drop the **-o** before a masculine noun: **el primer amor** *first love*, **en primer lugar** *in the first place*, **el tercer día** *the third day*.

From *11th* onwards, ordinal numbers are rarely used. Cardinal numbers are used instead and are placed after the noun, except when they refer to events, anniversaries and celebrations:

el piso dieciocho *the eighteenth storey*
el capítulo veinte *the twentieth chapter*
el siglo veintiuno *the twenty-first century*
el sesenta aniversario *the sixtieth anniversary*

Ordinal numbers aren't generally used for dates either, although in Latin America **primero** is used for the first of the month:

el uno/primero de marzo *(on the) 1st March*
el catorce de mayo *(on the) 14th May*

answers

answers to checkpoints

checkpoint 1 page 24

1 Perdone/¿Me permite? *2* usted; *3* Encantado; Os presento a mi colega.
4 soy; no soy; *5* señor; *6* muchas; De nada; No hay de qué. *7* commiserate;
8 ¡Bienvenidos/as! *9* Hasta mañana; Hasta pronto; Nos vemos más tarde.
10 a; *11* I am, they are, we are; *12* afternoon and early evening: approximately
midday until 9 pm; *13* hija; *14* Estáis en vuestra casa/Están en su casa. *15* (mi)
apellido; *16* tía; Este; *17* No pasa nada/Nada, hombre. *18* ¿no?; ¿verdad?
19 ¿Nos tuteamos? or Trátame/Háblame de tú. *20* ¿Puedo?

checkpoint 2 page 40

1 Estoy aprendiendo español/Aprendo español. *2* ¿no?; ¿ verdad? *3* viven;
4 una piscina; un parque infantil; una cancha de tenis; un campo de fútbol;
una cancha/pista/campo de baloncesto; *5* quién, cuál, por qué, qué, cuándo,
dónde, cómo, cuántos, cuánto; *6* ¿Cómo se llaman? *7* No tengo sed; ¿Tienes
frío/a? (Ella tiene) razón; Hoy no tengo prisa. *8* viud**o** – My grandfather is
a widower; gales**es** – My friends are Welsh; rubi**a** – My cousin is blonde;
trabajador**a** – My neighbour is very hard-working; simpátic**o** – My friend's
very nice. *9* en el noreste; cerca de York; entre la playa y la ciudad/el pueblo;
en primera línea de playa; *10* Antipático means nasty/mean, the others all
describe positive qualities. *11* outspoken; *12* ¿Dónde se encuentra su casa en
Valencia?; *13* contaminado; *14* trigo; *15* ancho/estrecho; montañoso/llano;
limpio/sucio; ruidoso/tranquilo; viejo/nuevo

checkpoint 3 page 52

1 microbiólogo/laboratorio, mecánico/taller de coches, docente/universidad,
cocinera/restaurante, enfermero/hospital; Un canguro is a nanny. *2* I'm a
doctor; We're dentists; She's a civil servant. *3* desde hace; *4* arqueólogo,
meteorólogo; rheumatologist, sociologist, Egyptologist; *5* fontanero;
6 trabajador(a), currante; *7 a* desde casa; *b* a tiempo parcial; *c* a tiempo
completo; *8* Mi compañero/a es trabajador/a autónomo/a. *9* Estoy
desempleado/a. *10* in retail; in the public sector; in the health sector; in a
factory; *11* ¿Cuál es tu/su puesto de trabajo? *12* tú; vosotros/as; usted; usted;
13 a gestiono; *b* hago; *c* dirijo; *14* Me ocupo de la página web de la empresa.
15 Trabajaba como analista; Era cocinero; Juan trabajaba en una consulta
médica.

checkpoint 4 page 64

1 Disculpa/Disculpe. *2* ¿Me entiendes? ¿Me explico? *3* qué; *4* ¿Cómo se dice 'crisis' en español? *5* en; *6* irritation; It means What a mess! *7* Tengo alergia al trigo y a los productos lácteos. *8* disarm, undress, undo, dehumanize; *9* ¡Qué casualidad! positive; ¡Qué asco! negative; ¡Qué alegría! positive; ¡Qué lástima! negative; *10* ¿Te/Le importaría explicarlo? *11* aún, todavía, total; *12* ¿Qué quiere decir salmorejo?/¿Qué significa salmorejo? (It's very similar to gazpacho.) *13* por ejemplo; *14* algo; *15* split the bill; *16* Tengo hambre. *17* ¡Qué suerte tienes! *18* bien; se; *19* calimocho; *20* Lo tengo en la punta de la lengua.

checkpoint 5 page 80

1 You use the imperfect. *2* ser and ir; *3* prohibido, dejado, logrado, cogido; *4* Autobús is used in Spain, the others only in Latin America. *5* cada semana; *6* Recientemente he comprado una guitarra. *7* He perdido mi pasaporte y mis llaves. *8* Ha habido un accidente en la calle. *9* ayer por la noche, anoche; *10* I've just done it, I used to do it; Acabamos de hacerlo, Solíamos hacerlo; *11* the day before yesterday, the other day; *12* Tenía doce años cuando conocí a Ana. *13* ¿Habías leído el libro antes de ver la película? *14* I am thinking about, I was thinking about; *15* no he visto, han llegado, ¿Habéis estado antes?, No hemos estado nunca.

checkpoint 6 page 92

1 La natación, swimming, is not a ball game. *2* Nos gusta muchísimo la habitación. *3* ¿(A ella) le gustan los videojuegos?; ¿(A ellos) les gustan los videojuegos? *4* No me gusta esquiar. *5* No me van/No me hacen mucha gracia/No me gustan para nada/No me gustan de ninguna manera las telenovelas. *6* Habla como un loro. *7* me ha gustado; *8* vinos preferidos, regiones preferidas, museos preferidos, música preferida, películas preferidas, fotos preferidas; *9* ¿Te gusta cocinar? *10* usted prefiere, vosotros/as preferís and tú prefieres; *11* Les encanta correr/Les gusta muchísimo correr/Les chifla correr. *12* para nada, de ninguna manera; *13* siempre; *14* (A él) no le interesan tus/sus ideas. *15* mejor; *16* de ninguna manera, muy poco, poco, bastante, mucho, muchísimo, con locura; *17* No me gusta mucho madrugar, No me gusta para nada/de ninguna manera hacer bricolaje, Prefiero viajar.

checkpoint 7 page 106

1 jueves, sábado; mayo, junio, julio; *2* See you on the eleventh, See you at eleven o'clock; *3* viaje, vuelo, día; *4* ¿Os apetece dar un paseo por el casco antiguo? *5* Es una lástima. *6* We're meeting on Thursday. *7* Igualmente. *8* el primero/uno de mayo, el seis de enero, el treinta y uno de diciembre; *9* ¿Por qué no vamos al cine? *10* tomemos let's take, vamos let's go, hagamos let's

make/do; *11* está; *12* hacía/hizo frío, estaba/estuvo nublado; *13* viene;
14 Os esperaría si pudiera. *15* if only, I wish; *16* Mil gracias. Ha sido una tarde
estupenda. *17* De buena gana/Con mucho gusto/Me gustaría mucho. ¿Pero
cuándo se celebra la fiesta?

checkpoint 8 page 124

1 I must start now, I ought to start now. *2* Me apeteció hacerlo (I fancied
doing it). The others all suggest that you were obliged to do something. *3* Luis
tiene que marcharse/irse y quiere hacer una foto de grupo. *4* Cuando era más
joven, conocía bastante bien Edimburgo. *5* Debe de tener cincuenta años.
6 ¿Tenéis ganas de visitar Sevilla? *7* ¿Le importa si cierro la puerta? *8* I'd like to
learn: quisiera/quería/querría/me gustaría aprender; I ought to learn: debería
aprender; I must learn: debo aprender; I want to learn: quiero aprender; I
need to learn: tengo que aprender; I fancy learning: me apetece/tengo ganas
de aprender; *9* A Adam le gustaría trabajar en España, pero Julia no quiere
vivir en el extranjero. *10* ¿Sabes dónde vive el joven que conocimos ayer? Sé
que vive por aquí, pero no conozco bien el barrio. *11* They all involve money
transactions. *12* people you might know; *13* leer, llamar, lograr, llorar, llegar;
14 El año pasado debíamos de haber hecho un crucero, pero tuvimos que
cancelar la reserva. *15* Siempre he querido viajar.

checkpoint 9 page 138

1 your opinion; a su juicio, a su parecer, en su opinión; *2* en segundo lugar;
total que, en resumen; *3* Genial; Estoy totalmente de acuerdo. *4* el terrorismo,
el capitalismo, el socialismo, el optimismo; *5* No coincidimos en este aspecto.
6 dado que, puesto que; *7* it is; *8* a haya; b lleguen; c venga; d era; *9* haber;
10 no creo que; *11* quinientos; it's the only cardinal number (1, 2, 3), as
distinct from ordinal numbers such as first, second, third; *12* Óscar; el más
joven; *13* cada vez menos difícil; cada vez más fácil; *14* centenares/cientos;
15 seven point five per cent, zero point eight percent

checkpoint 10 page 153

1 ¿Falta algo? *2* on a computer keyboard; *3* ¡Aprovéchate!, ¡Aprovéchense!
4 ¿Tienen/Hay wifi?; ¿Cuál es la contraseña? *5* rung the wrong number; *6* Hay
mucha gente, Habrá mucha gente, Había mucha gente; *7* lo; *8* gadget, news,
signal (coverage), file, dose, mouse, goose barnacle, light, network; *9* se;
10 Prueba estas almendras, Ten cuidado, Apresúrate, No te preocupes;
Probad estas almendras, Tened cuidado, Apresuraos, No os preocupéis.
11 Echo mucho de menos a mi amiga Sofía. *12* No olvides hacerlo/No te
olvides de hacerlo, No olvide hacerlo/No se olvide de hacerlo, No olvidéis
hacerlo/No os olvidéis de hacerlo. *13* He perdido mi memoria USB, Tenemos
que/Debemos comprar un cargador. *14* a escribiré I will write, guglearé I will

google; *b* nos hemos despedido we've said goodbye, hemos apagado we've switched off; *c* buscaron they looked for, encendieron they switched on; *15* Ha sido un placer conocerte/conocerle/conoceros/conocerles.

answers to verb practice

verb practice 1 page 39

1   *a* estoy; *b* somos; *c* es; *d* son; *e* estáis; *f* está; *g* soy; *h* es; *i* son; *j* eres

2   *a* tengo; tiene; *b* tiene; *c* tiene; *d* tenemos; *e* tienes; *f* tenéis; *g* tienen; *h* tiene

3   *a* ¿(Ella) es canadiense o americana? *b* ¿Son hermanas Marta y Conchi? *c* ¿El hotel tiene una piscina? *d* Pablo es gay, ¿verdad? *e* ¿Tienes/Tiene/Tenéis/Tienen sed? *f* ¿Hay pistas de tenis?

verb practice 2 page 51

1   *a* tú esperas; *b* ustedes cambian; *c* vosotros/as compráis; *d* dura; *e* nosotros/as ponemos; *f* usted vende; *g* yo como; *h* ella vive; *i* nosotros/as escribimos; *j* yo abro

2   *a* hago; *b* haces; *c* hace; *d* hace; *e* hacemos; *f* hacen; *g* hace

3   *a* se; *b* se; *c* nos; *d* se; *e* te; *f* se; *g* os

verb practice 3 page 79

1   *a* tú querías; *b* nosotros/as teníamos; *c* usted iba; *d* ellos/as se bañaban; *e* yo hacía; *f* nosotros/as charlábamos; *g* ustedes eran; *h* vosotros/as leíais

2   *a* has; *b* ha; *c* han; *d* ha; *e* han; *f* he; *g* hemos; *h* ha; *i* han

3   *a* Lo hice. *b* Ellos compraron un coche. *c* ¿Pagaste la cuenta? *d* Murió el alcalde. *e* Arreglamos el problema.

4   *a* estaba, estábamos, me caí; I was with Juan; we were in the square and I fell over. *b* nació, vivía, tenían; She was born in 1964; as a child, she lived in Galicia where her grandparents had a hotel-restaurant. *c* fuiste, conoció; Did you go to the town/village where your mother met your father?

verb practice 4 page 105

1   *a* tú contestarás you will reply; *b* ellos irán they will go; *c* vosotros tomaréis you will take; *d* durará it will last; *e* nosotros pondremos we will put; *f* usted olvidará you will forget; *g* yo lograré I will succeed; *h* ella

hará she will make/do; *i* nosotros llegaremos we will arrive; *j* tú estarás you will be; *k* yo seré I will be; *l* habrá there will be

2   *a* tú contestarías you would reply; *b* ellos irían they would go; *c* vosotros tomaríais you would take; *d* duraría it would last; *e* nosotros pondríamos we would put; *f* usted olvidaría you would forget; *g* yo lograría I would succeed; *h* ella haría she would make/do; *i* nosotros llegaríamos we would arrive; *j* tú estarías you would be; *k* yo sería I would be; *l* habría there would be

3   *a* future; we will win; *b* future; you will want; *c* past; she has called; *d* present; they study/are studying; *e* present; you want; *f* conditional; they would change; *g* future; we will prefer; *h* conditional; we would prefer; *i* past; there was; *j* present; I do/make

4   *a* vi; *b* iii; *c* v; *d* i; *e* vii; *f* iv; *g* ii

verb practice 5 page 123

1   tener que/deber: ought, was supposed to, must, should have, had to, used to have to; querer: wanted to, would like to; poder: may, could, used to be able to, can

3   *a* usted debe; vosotros/as debéis; *b* nosotros/as queremos; él/ella quiere; *c* ellos/ellas deben; yo debo; *d* él/ella puede; yo puedo; *e* tú quieres; ellos/ellas quieren; *f* vosotros/as podéis; nosotros/as podemos; *g* tú debes; nosotros/as debemos; *h* él/ella puede; ellos/ellas pueden; *i* yo quiero; vosotros/as queréis

4   conditional: *a* usted debería; vosotros/as deberíais; *b* nosotros/as querríamos; él/ella querría; *c* ellos/ellas deberían; yo debería; *d* él/ella podría; yo podría; *e* tú querrías; ellos/ellas querrían; *f* vosotros/as podríais; nosotros/as podríamos; *g* tú deberías; nosotros/as deberíamos; *h* él/ella podría; ellos/ellas podrían; *i* yo querría; vosotros/as querríais

   imperfect: *a* usted debía; vosotros/as debíais; *b* nosotros/as queríamos; él/ella quería; *c* ellos/ellas debían; yo debía; *d* él/ella podía; yo podía; *e* tú querías; ellos/ellas querían; *f* vosotros/as podíais; nosotros/as podíamos; *g* tú debías; nosotros/as debíamos; *h* él/ella podía; ellos/ellas podían; *i* yo quería; vosotros/as queríais

   preterite: *a* usted debió; vosotros/as debisteis; *b* nosotros/as quisimos; él/ella quiso; *c* ellos/ellas debieron; yo debí; *d* él/ella pudo; yo pude; *e* tú quisiste; ellos/ellas quisieron; *f* vosotros/as pudisteis; nosotros/as pudimos; *g* tú debiste; nosotros/as debimos; *h* él/ella pudo; ellos/ellas pudieron; *i* yo quise; vosotros/as quisisteis

vocabulary builder

Nouns ending in **-o** are masculine and those ending in **-a** are feminine unless indicated otherwise. The gender of all other nouns is included: m, f or m/f.

Adjectives are listed with their masculine singular ending (page 159).

Verbs are in the infinitive; irregular past participles pp are included.

A
A&E Department urgencias
able capaz
able: to be able poder
to abolish abolir
about sobre
above encima
abroad extranjero
to abstain abstenerse
to accelerate acelerar
to accept aceptar
access acceso
accessible bien comunicado
accessory accesorio
accident accidente (m)
to accompany acompañar
accountant contable (m/f)
to accuse acusar
active activo
activity actividad (f)
actor, actress actor (m), actriz (f)
acupuncture acupuntura
to add añadir
address dirección (f)
to adjust arreglar
to admire admirar
to adopt adoptar
advantage ventaja

adventure aventura
advertisement anuncio
advice consejo
advisable aconsejable
to advise aconsejar
aeroplane avión (m)
affectionate cariñoso
afraid: to be afraid tener miedo
after después
afternoon tarde (f)
afterwards después
against contra
age edad (f)
agency agencia
aggressive agresivo
ago hace
to agree estar de acuerdo
agricultural agrícola
air conditioning aire acondicionado (m)
air traffic controller controlador(a) aéreo/a
airy aireado, ventilado
all todo
allergic alérgico
to alleviate aliviar
to allow permitir, admitir
almost casi
already ya
also también
although aunque

always siempre
American americano/a
amusing divertido
to analyse analizar
ancient antiguo
and y
ankle tobillo
to announce anunciar
to annoy enfadar, fastidiar, molestar
annoying molesto
to annul anular
another otro
to answer contestar, responder
antique (adj) antiguo
anxiety ansiedad (f)
anxious nervioso
any algún/alguna
anything algo
anyway de todas maneras
apartment piso, apartamento
aperitif aperitivo
apology disculpa
to appear aparecer
appearance aspecto, apariencia
to applaud aplaudir
to apply aplicar
to appreciate apreciar
appropriate adecuado, conveniente

aqueduct acueducto
archery tiro con arco
architecture arquitectura
area zona
Argentinean argentino
arm brazo
arms (military) armas (f pl)
aromatic aromático
around por
to arrange colocar
to arrange to meet quedar
to arrive llegar
art arte (f)
arthritis artritis (f)
artistic artístico
to ask a question preguntar
to ask for pedir
asparagus espárrago
aspect aspecto
to assault asaltar
to assure asegurar
at a, en
atrocity barbaridad (f)
attachment (email) archivo adjunto
attack atentado
to attend asistir
to attend to atender
attention atención (f); to pay attention fijarse
attic ático
attitude actitud (f)
to attract atraer
attraction atracción (f)
aunt tía
austerity austeridad (f)
to authorize autorizar
Autonomous Region Comunidad Autónoma

autumn otoño
available disponible
avenue avenida
average media
to avoid evitar
awful: I feel awful me siento fatal

B
babysitter niñero/a
back espalda
to back up (IT) hacer copia de seguridad
backache dolor de espalda
bad (adj) malo
bad (adv) mal; I feel bad me siento mal
balanced equilibrado
balcony balcón (m)
bald calvo
bank banco
banker banquero/a
bar bar (m)
barbecue barbacoa
basic básico, sencillo
basketball baloncesto
to bathe bañar(se)
bathroom baño
to be estar, ser (pp sido)
to be able poder
to be born nacer
to be careful tener cuidado
beach playa
beans alubias
to beat batir
beautiful bonito, precioso, guapo, hermoso
because porque
bed cama

bed: to go to bed acostarse
bedroom dormitorio
beep señal (f)
before antes
beforehand con antelación
to begin comenzar, empezar
beginning principio; at the beginning al principio
to believe creer
belly barriga
belt cinturón (m)
to bend doblar
bend curva
best el/la mejor
better mejor
better: to get better mejorar
big grande
bike bici(cleta)
biological biológico
birth nacimiento
birthday cumpleaños
birthday card tarjeta de cumpleaños
black negro
block bloque (m)
blond rubio
blue azul
boat barco
body cuerpo; full-bodied con cuerpo
to boil cocer
bold atrevido
to book reservar
boots botas; walking boots botas de andar
to bore aburrir
bored/boring aburrido; to get bored aburrirse

to borrow pedir prestado
bow tie pajarita
boy chico
boyfriend novio
brave valiente
brazen atrevido
to break romper (pp roto)
break pausa
breakfast desayuno; to eat breakfast desayunar
breeze brisa
bridge puente (m)
briefcase maletín (m)
to bring traer (pp traído)
British británico
broad amplio
broken roto
brother hermano
brother-in-law cuñado
brown marrón
to browse (internet) navegar
to browse (look at) mirar
browser navegador (m)
budget presupuesto
to build construir
building edificio
building industry construcción (f)
bull toro; bullfighting toreo
bungee-jumping puenting (m)
burly robusto
bus autobús (m); bus stop parada de autobús
business negocio
bustling animado
busy concurrido

but pero
to buy comprar

C
cake tarta, pastel (m)
to calculate calcular
calendar calendario
to call llamar; to be called llamarse
calorie caloría
camera cámara de fotos
to camp acampar
campaign campaña
campsite campamento
can lata
can (to be able to) poder
to cancel cancelar
candidate candidato/a
canny astuto
canoeing piragüismo
capable hábil
capacity capacidad (f)
car coche (m); convertible descapotable
card tarjeta; credit card tarjeta de crédito
cashpoint cajero automático
cast (theatre) reparto
castle castillo
catastrophic desastroso
cathedral catedral (f)
to cause causar
cautious prudente
to celebrate celebrar
cellar (wine) bodega
central céntrico
centre centro
centrist del centro
century siglo

to change cambiar
change cambio
chaos caos (m)
to charge cargar
charger cargador (m)
charity organización (f) benéfica
charity work trabajo voluntario
charming encantador
chat charla, (online) chat (m)
to chat charlar, (online) chatear
cheap barato
to cheat engañar
to check comprobar
cheek mejilla
cheeky descarado
cheers salud·
cheese queso
chef cocinero/a
chemical químico
chemist farmacia
cherry cereza
chess ajedrez (m)
chest pecho
to chew masticar
chickpeas garbanzos
child niño/a
childhood infancia
childminder niñero/a
children hijos, niños
chin barbilla
to choose elegir, escoger
chop chuleta
chore tarea; household chores tareas domésticas
choreographer coreógrafo/a
Christmas Navidad (f)

church iglesia
cinema cine (m)
city ciudad (f)
Civil Guards Guardia Civil
civil servant funcionario/a
to clarify clarificar, aclarar
class clase (f)
classic(al) clásico
clean limpio
to clean limpiar
clearly claramente
clever inteligente, listo
to click hacer clic
client cliente (m/f)
climatic climático
to climb escalar
climbing escalada
cloakroom guardarropa (m); (toilet) aseo
to close cerrar
clothes ropa; warm
clothes ropa de abrigo
cloudy cubierto, nublado
coast costa
coat abrigo
coeliac celiaco
coffee café (m)
coffee maker cafetera
coincidence casualidad (f)
cold frío
cold (illness) resfriado
cold: to be cold tener frío
colleague colega (m/f), compañero/a
to collect recoger
colour color (m)
to comb peinar
to combat combatir

to come venir
comfortable cómodo
commitment compromiso, obligación (f)
to communicate comunicar
community comunitario
company empresa
to compare comparar
compartment compartimento
compass brújula
to compete competir, participar
competent capaz, competente
complex complejo
computer computadora, ordenador (m)
computer scientist informático/a
concert concierto
to condemn condenar
condition condición (f)
conference conferencia, congreso
confident seguro de sí mismo/a
to confirm confirmar
confirmation confirmación (f)
congested congestionado
to congratulate felicitar
congratulations enhorabuena
to connect conectar
to conserve conservar
to consider considerar
to consist of consistir en

construction worker albañil (m/f)
consultant consultor(a), especialista (m/f), asesor(a)
to contact contactar
contact contacto
to contain contener
to continue seguir, continuar
contract contrato
to contribute contribuir
to control controlar
convenient cómodo
to convince convencer
to cook cocinar
cook cocinero/a
cool fresco
to cool resfriarse
to coordinate coordinar
to cost costar
cosy acogedor(a)
cot cuna, camita
cotton algodón (m)
cough tos (f)
to cough toser
counsellor asesor(a)
to count contar
country país (m)
couple par (m), pareja
course curso
course (of) claro, por supuesto
cousin primo/a
to cover cubrir (pp cubierto)
cramped estrecho
to crash chocar, colisionar
to crash (IT) colgarse
crazy loco
cream pomada
to create crear

creative creativo
crèche guardería
credit crédito; credit card tarjeta de crédito
to criticise criticar
to cross cruzar, atravesar
crossword crucigrama (m)
crowded concurrido
cruise crucero
to cry llorar
cuisine cocina
cultivated culto
culture cultura
to cure curar
curiosity curiosidad (f)
curly rizado
to cut cortar

D
daft tonto
dairy products productos lácteos
to dance bailar
dance baile (m)
to dare osar, atreverse
dark oscuro; dark hair moreno
date fecha
dated anticuado
daughter hija
daughter-in-law nuera
day día (m)
dead muerto
dear querido, estimado
to decide decidir
deckchair tumbona
to decorate decorar
dedicated dedicado
to defend defender
delay retraso
to delete borrar
delicate delicado

delicious delicioso, rico
to delight encantar
delightful encantador
demanding exigente
to demonstrate demostrar
demonstrator manifestante (m/f)
dentist dentista (m/f)
to depart salir
department departamento
department store grandes almacenes (m pl)
to depend depender
deposit fianza
depressed deprimido
to describe describir
to deserve merecer
designer diseñador(a)
dessert postre (m)
destination destino
to destroy destruir
development urbanización (f)
diabetic diabético
diarrhoea diarrea
to die morir (pp muerto)
diet dieta, régimen (m)
different diferente
difficult difícil
difficulty dificultad (f)
dilapidated deteriorado
dining room comedor
dinner cena; to eat dinner cenar
diplomatic discreto
to direct dirigir
direction dirección (f); in direction of en dirección a
dirty sucio

disagreeable antipático
to disappear desaparecer
disappointing decepcionante
disappointment desilusión (f)
discount descuento
to discover descubrir (pp descubierto)
to discuss discutir, hablar de
disgust asco
dish plato
dishwasher lavaplatos (m), lavavajillas (m)
distance distancia
to distract distraer
to distribute distribuir
to disturb molestar
divine divino
diving buceo
divorced divorciado
DIY bricolaje (m)
to do hacer (pp hecho)
doctor doctor(a), médico/a
document documento
dog perro
dolphin delfín
donkey burro
dosage dosis (f)
dot punto; on the dot en punto
double doble
to doubt dudar
to download descargar
to drain escurrir
to draw (tie) empatar
to dream soñar
to dress vestir; to get dressed vestirse
dress vestido
to drink beber, tomar

to drive conducir
driver chófer (m/f)
driving licence carné de conducir (m)
to drizzle lloviznar
to drown ahogar(se)
dry seco, árido
to dry secar
dryer secadora
dumb tonto
during durante
dynamic dinámico

E
ear oído, oreja
early temprano, pronto
to earn ganar
east este (m)
Easter Pascua
easy fácil
to eat comer
economic económico
to edit editar
educational educativo
effective eficaz
efficient eficaz, eficiente
egg huevo
elderly (the) mayores (m/f pl)
to elect elegir
election elección (f)
electric eléctrico
electrician electricista (m/f)
to eliminate eliminar
email correo electrónico
emotion emoción (f)
to emphasise enfatizar
to encounter encontrar(se)
to end terminar

end fin (m), final (m); at the end of al final de
engagement compromiso
engineer ingeniero/a
England Inglaterra
English inglés(a)
to enjoy disfrutar
to enjoy oneself divertirse
to enter entrar
to entertain entretener
to entrust encargar
to envy envidiar
equator ecuador
equipped equipado
especially especialmente, sobre todo
to establish establecer
estate agency agencia inmobiliaria
estate agent agente (m/f) inmobiliario/a
European europeo
evening tarde (f), noche (f)
event evento
every todo/a, cada
everything todo
to exaggerate exagerar
example ejemplo; for example por ejemplo
to exceed exceder
excellent excelente
to exchange intercambiar
exciting emocionante
excursión excursión (f)
to excuse disculpar
exercise ejercicio
exhausted acabado, agotado

exhibition exposición (f), muestra
to exist existir
expensive caro
experience experiencia
to explain explicar
to explore explorar
exquisite exquisito
to extend extender
extreme extremo; extreme sports deportes extremos
extremism extremismo
eye ojo

F
fabric tejido
face cara
facing orientado
fact: in fact en realidad, de hecho
to fail fallar
faithful fiel
to fake fingir, simular
to fall caerse
to fall in love enamorarse
false falso
family familia
famous famoso
fantastic fantástico
far lejos
farming agricultura
fascinating fascinante
fashion moda
fast rápido, rápidamente
to fast ayunar
fat gordo
father padre
father-in-law suegro
favourite preferido
fear miedo

to fear temer(se)
fee tarifa
to feel sentirse
to feel like tener ganas (de)
festival fiesta (f), festival (m)
fever fiebre (f)
fiancé(e) novio/a
field campo
to fight pelearse, combatir
file archivo
to fill llenar
to fill in rellenar
film película
to find encontrar, hallar
finger dedo
to finish acabar, terminar
fire fuego, incendio
fire fighter bombero/a
fire place chimenea
first primero
first aid kit botiquín (m)
fish pescado
to fish pescar
to fit quedar
to fix fijar
flat plano, llano
flat (appartment) piso
flight vuelo
flight attendant auxiliar (m/f) de vuelo
air stewardess azafata (f)
floor planta
flu gripe (f)
fluent fluido
to fly volar
to focus enfocar
fog niebla
folder carpeta
to follow seguir

following siguiente
food comida
food product alimento
food shopping compra
foot pie (m); on foot a pie
football fútbol (m); five a side fútbol sala
footballer futbolista (m/f)
footwear calzado
for para, por
for (time) para, desde hace
to forbid prohibir
forehead frente (f)
foreign extranjero
to forget olvidar
form formulario
fortnight quince días
fortunately afortunadamente
founded fundado
frankly francamente
freedom libertad (f)
freelance autónomo
to freeze (IT) colgarse
freezer congelador (m)
fridge frigorífico
friend amigo/a
friendly amable, amistoso
from de, desde
frustration frustración (f)
to fry freír
frying pan sartén (f)
full completo, lleno
full time a tiempo completo
fun: to have fun divertirse
furthermore además

G
gadget chisme (m)
gale vendaval (m)
gallery galería
gambling juego (de apuestas)
garage garaje (m)
garden jardín (m)
to garden cuidar el jardín
gardening jardinería
garlic ajo
garment prenda
gastronomic gastronómico
generally por lo/en general
generous generoso
genetics genética
to get (obtain) adquirir
to get off bajarse
to get up levantarse; to get up early levantarse temprano, madrugar
gifted dotado
gig concierto
girl chica
girlfriend novia
to give dar
glacier glaciar (m)
glass vaso
glasses gafas (f pl); sunglasses gafas de sol
gloves guantes (m pl)
to go ir
to go away irse, marcharse
to go back volver
to go down descender
to go out salir
to go up subir
golf course campo de golf
good buen, bueno

good looking guapo, atractivo
goose oca
gothic gótico
government gobierno
to grab agarrar
to graduate graduarse
graduation graduación (f)
grandchildren nietos
granddaughter nieta
grandfather abuelo
grandmother abuela
grandparents abuelos
grandson nieto
graphic gráfico
great estupendo
green verde
to greet saludar
greetings saludos
grey gris
grilled a la plancha
gross asqueroso
ground floor planta baja
group grupo
to grow crecer
to growl gruñir
to guarantee garantizar
to guess adivinar
guide guía (m/f); tourist guide guía turístico/a
guidebook guía (f)
guided guiado
guitar guitarra
gym gimnasio

H
to haggle regatear
hair pelo
half mitad (f)
hand mano (f); by hand a mano
hand made artesano

handbag bolso
handball balonmano
handle asa
handsome guapo
handy práctico
hangover resaca
to happen pasar, ocurrir
happy contento, feliz, alegre
hard fuerte
harmony armonía
hashtag almohadilla
hat sombrero
to hate odiar
hateful odioso
to have tener, haber
to have to deber, tener que
hayfever alergia al polen
he él
head cabeza
headache dolor (m) de cabeza
health salud (f)
healthy sano
to hear oír
to heat calentar
heat calor (m)
heating calefacción (f)
helmet casco
to help ayudar
help ayuda
Help! ¡Socorro!
here aquí
to hide esconder
hip cadera
to hire alquilar
hire alquiler (m); hire car coche (m) de alquiler
historian historiador(a)

historic histórico
history historia
to hit golpear
hobby afición (f)
holidays vacaciones (f)
holistic holístico
home domicilio
honest honesto, sincero
to hope esperar
horrendous horrendo
horrible horrible
horse caballo
hot caliente
hot (to be hot) tener calor
hour hora
house casa
housewife ama de casa
how cómo; how? ¿cómo?
how many? ¿cuántos/as?
how much? ¿cuánto/a?
however pero, sin embargo
to hug abrazar
hug abrazo
huge enorme
human rights derechos humanos
humid húmedo
hundreds cientos
hunger hambre (f); to be hungry tener hambre
to hurry apresurarse; to be in a hurry tener prisa
to hurt (be in pain) doler
to hurt (damage) hacer daño

to hurt oneself hacerse daño
husband marido
hydrotherapy hidroterapia

I
I yo
icon icono
ID DNI, identificación (f), carné (m) de identidad
idea idea; good idea buena idea
to identify identificar
if si
to imitate imitar
immaculate inmaculado
impact golpe (m)
impeccable impecable
impetuous impetuoso
important importante
imposing grandioso
impossible imposible
impressive impresionante
to improve mejorar
in en
inbox bandeja de entrada
to include incluir
inconsiderate desconsiderado
to increase aumentar
increase subida
incredible increíble
to indicate indicar
industrial industrial
industry industria, sector (m)
to influence influir
information información (f)

ingredient ingrediente (m)
inland en el interior
inside interior (m)
inside (prep) dentro (de)
to insist insistir
instead en cambio
insurance seguro
interest interés (m)
to interest interesar
interested interesado
interesting interesante
intermediate intermedio
international internacional
to interview entrevistar
intolerance intolerancia
to introduce presentar
to invite invitar
Irish irlandés/irlandesa
iron hierro; to iron planchar
irregularity irregularidad (f)
irresponsible irresponsable
irritated: to get irritated irritarse
island isla
IT informática

J
jacket chaqueta
jeans vaqueros (m pl)
job advert anuncio de trabajo
jogging hacer footing
joke broma
to joke bromear
journalist periodista
journey viaje (m)
joy alegría

jumper jersey (m), suéter (m)

K
kayaking piragüismo
to keep fit mantenerse en forma
key llave (f)
key (IT) tecla
to key in teclear
keyboard (IT) teclado
kind amable, simpático
kind-hearted generoso
to kiss besar
kisses besos
kitchen cocina
knee rodilla
to know (fact) saber
to know (person/place) conocer

L
to lack faltar
landscape paisaje (m)
language idioma (m), lengua
laptop portátil (m)
large grande, amplio
to last durar
last (final) último
last (past) pasado
late tarde (adv)
latest último
Latin America Latinoamérica
to laugh reír, reírse
lazy perezoso
leaflet folleto
to learn aprender
leather piel (f)
to leave dejar
to leave (go out) salir
to leave (something) dejar

lecturer docente, profesor universitario
left izquierda; on the left a la izquierda
left wing de izquierda(s)
leg pierna
leisure activity diversión (f)
to lend prestar
Lent Cuaresma
less menos
lesson clase (f)
letter carta
level nivel (m)
to lie (untruth) mentir
life vida
lifeguard salvavidas (m/f), socorrista (m/f)
to lift levantar
lift ascensor (m)
light luminoso
light luz (f)
lightweight ligero
like como
to like gustar
likeable simpático
likely seguramente
linen lino
list lista
to listen escuchar
little pequeño; a little un poco
to live vivir
lively animado
living room sala de estar
to load cargar
lobster langosta
located situado
lock cerradura
long largo
to look mirar

to look after ocuparse de, cuidar (de)
to look for buscar
to look like parecer, parecerse a
lorry driver camionero/a
to lose perder
to lose weight adelgazar, perder peso
lot (a lot) mucho/a (adj), mucho (adv)
to love encantar, querer
lovely bonito
to lower bajar
loyal fiel
luck suerte (f)
lucky afortunado
luggage equipaje (m)
lunch comida, almuerzo; to eat lunch comer, almorzar
luxurious de lujo, lujoso

M
mad loco
magnificent magnífico
to maintain mantener
maintenance mantenimiento
majority mayoría
to make hacer (pp hecho)
malfunction trastorno
man hombre (m)
to manage (business) gestionar
to manage (succeed) lograr, conseguir
manager gerente (m/f)
manufacture fabricación (f)

map mapa (m), plano
marine marino
market mercado
married casado
to marry casarse
martial arts artes marciales (f pl)
marvellous maravilloso
masterpiece obra de arte
match partido
mature maduro
to mature madurar
to mean significar
mean antipático
meat carne (f)
mediaeval medieval
medicine medicina
meditation meditación (f)
Mediterranean mediterráneo
medium mediano
medium dry semiseco
to meet encontrarse, reunirse, conocer
meeting reunión (f)
memory stick memoria USB
to mend arreglar
mess lío, caos (m)
message mensaje (m)
microwave microondas (m)
migraine migraña
minimum mínimo
minority minoría
minute minuto
to miss extrañar, echar de menos
misunderstanding malentendido
to mix mezclar

mobile móvil (m)
model (fashion) modelo (m/f)
modern moderno
money dinero
to monitor controlar
month mes (m)
monument monumento
more más
morning mañana
mother madre (f)
mother-in-law suegra
motor racing automovilismo
motorbike moto (f)
mountain montaña
mountaineering montañismo, alpinismo
mountainous montañoso
mouse ratón (m)
moustache bigote (m)
mouth boca
to move cambiarse, mover(se)
move traslado
to move (relocate) mudarse
moving emocionante
MP diputado/a
muddy fangoso, embarrado
multinational multinacional
mum madre, mamá
muscular musculoso
museum museo
music música
musician músico/a
my mi, mis

N
naïve ingenuo
name nombre (m)
nanny (babysitter) niñero/a, canguro (m/f)
nap (afternoon) siesta
narrow estrecho
nasty antipático, desagradable
nationality nacionalidad (f)
nature naturaleza
nausea asco
near cerca
necessary necesario; to be necessary hacer falta
neck cuello
to need hacer falta, necesitar
to neglect descuidar
neighbour vecino
neighbourhood barrio
neither... nor ni... ni
never nunca
new nuevo
New Year's Eve Nochevieja
next próximo
nice simpático, majo, bonito
night noche (f)
nightclub discoteca
nobody nadie
noisy ruidoso
none ninguno/a
nonsense tontería, disparate (m)
normally normalmente
north norte (m)
nose nariz (f)
not at all en absoluto
nothing nada

now ahora
nuisance lata
number número
nurse enfermero/a
nutrition alimentación (f)

O
object objeto
to obstruct obstruir
to obtain adquirir
obviously obviamente
ocean océano
odd curioso
of de
to offer ofrecer
offer oferta
office oficina
office worker oficinista (m/f)
often muchas veces, a menudo
oil aceite (m); olive oil aceite de oliva
OK vale, de acuerdo
old antiguo, viejo; old town casco antiguo/ viejo
old-fashioned anticuado
omelette tortilla
one uno/a
only solamente, solo
to open abrir (pp abierto)
open abierto
opening apertura
opera ópera
operetta zarzuela
opinion opinión (f), parecer (m)
opportunity oportunidad (f)
to oppose oponer(se)

optician oculista (m/f)
optimistic optimista
orange naranja
to organise organizar
organiser organizador(a)
original original
other otro/a
our nuestro/a/os/as
outpatient's clinic ambulatorio
outside exterior
outskirts afueras
outspoken franco
oven horno
over there allí
to owe deber
owner dueño/a
oyster ostra

P
PA secretario/a de dirección
pace ritmo; pace of life ritmo de vida
packed lleno, a tope
padlock candado
page página
pain dolor (m)
painkiller analgésico, calmante (m)
to paint pintar
parachuting paracaidismo
paragliding parapente (m)
parents padres (m pl)
to park aparcar
park parque (m); children's park parque infantil
parking aparcamiento
part parte (f)
part time a tiempo parcial

partner compañero/a
party (political) partido
passenger pasajero/a
passport pasaporte (m)
password contraseña
path sendero
patient paciente
to pay pagar
to pay attention fijarse
peace paz (f)
peanut cacahuete (m)
penguin pingüino
people gente (f sing)
pepper pimiento
perfect perfecto
perfection perfección (f)
performance espectáculo; live performance espectáculo en vivo
person persona
personally personalmente to
persuade persuadir
pessimistic pesimista
petrol gasolina
pharmacist farmacéutico/a
pharmacy farmacia
to phone llamar por teléfono
photo foto (f)
physical físico
physically físicamente
physiotherapy fisioterapia
picturesque pintoresco
piece trozo
pilot piloto (m/f)
pity lástima
place lugar (m)
to plan planear
plan plan (m)

planet planeta (m)
plant planta
to play (game, sports) jugar (a)
to play (instrument) tocar
pleasant agradable, amable
pleasure placer (m)
plot of land parcela
plumber fontanero/a
plump gordito, rollizo
pocket bolsillo
police officer agente (m/f), policía (m/f)
police station comisaría
policy política
polite educado
politician político/a
politics política
poll encuesta
polluted contaminado
possibility posibilidad (f)
possible posible
postcard postal (f)
postman/woman cartero/a
to postpone posponer
potato patata
potholing espeleología
to pour echar
power poder (m)
practical práctico
practice práctica
to practise practicar
to prefer preferir
preferably preferiblemente
to prepare preparar
present regalo
to pretend fingir, simular
price precio

principle principio
to print imprimir
printer impresora
probably probablemente
problem problema (m)
to produce producir
product producto
profession profesión (f)
to programme programar
programmer programador(a)
to promise prometer
promotion ascenso
property vivienda
to propose proponer
to protest protestar
province provincia
public relations relaciones (f pl) públicas
pure puro
purse cartera, monedero
to put poner (pp puesto)
to put weight on engordar
puzzle rompecabezas (m)

Q
quality calidad (f)
question pregunta
quick rápido
quickly rápidamente
quiet tranquilo

R
radio radio (f)
rain lluvia
to rain llover; it's raining llueve
raincoat chubasquero

rarely raramente
rash impetuoso
rather bastante
to read leer
to realise (make happen) realizar
realistic razonable
rear trasero
reason razón (f)
to receive recibir
recently recientemente
recipe receta
to recommend aconsejar, recomendar
to rectify corregir
red rojo
red hair pelirrojo
red wine vino tinto
reference referencia
refugee refugiado
refurbished reformado
to refuse negar(se), rechazar
region región (f)
to relate to relacionarse con
to relax relajarse
reliable fiable, serio
relief alivio
remedy remedio
to remember acordarse de, recordar
to remind of recordar a
remote lejano
to remove quitar
to rent alquilar
to repeat repetir
to reply contestar, responder
to report to the police poner una denuncia
representative representante (m/f)

researcher investigador(a)
reservation reserva
resistant resistente
resort centro turístico
to respect respetar
to rest descansar
restaurant restaurante (m)
to restore restaurar
to retire jubilarse
retired jubilado
to return volver (pp vuelto), regresar
rice arroz (m)
rich rico
ridiculous ridículo, absurdo
riding equitación (f)
right derecha; on the right a la derecha
right wing de derecha(s)
right: to be right tener razón
ripen maduro
to ripen madurar
risk riesgo
to risk arriesgar
river río
road carretera
rocky pedregoso
room habitación (f), sala
rosé wine rosado
rough accidentado
round here por aquí
route camino, ruta
rowing remo
rubbish basura; empty the rubbish tirar la basura
rucksack mochila
rude maleducado

rugged accidentado
to run correr
run down deteriorado
to run through
atravesar
rural rural
to rush apresurar(se)
rustic rústico

S
sad triste
to sail navegar
sailing vela
salad ensalada
salary salario
sanction sanción (f)
sandwich bocadillo
sandy arenoso
satisfying agradable,
satisfactorio
to save ahorrar
to say decir (pp dicho)
school colegio, escuela,
instituto
science ciencia
scientist científico/a
to score marcar
Scotland Escocia
to scream chillar
screen monitor (m),
pantalla
scruffy descuidado
scuba diving buceo
sea mar (m)
seafood marisco(s)
seafood restaurant
marisquería
seafront primera línea
to search buscar
search engine buscador
seat plaza
secret secreto
secretary secretario/a
sector sector (m)

security vigilancia
security guard guardia
(m/f) de seguridad
to see ver (pp visto)
to seem parecer
self-employed
autónomo
selfish egoísta
to sell vender
to send enviar, mandar
sensitive sensible
separately aparte
to serve servir
to settle on quedar
to share compartir
she ella
shellfish marisco
ship barco
shirt camisa
shoes zapatos; shoe
shop zapatería
shop tienda
shopping compras;
to go shopping ir de
compras
short bajo, corto
shoulder hombro
show espectáculo
to shower ducharse
shower (weather)
chubasco
shrewd astuto
to shut cerrar
side lado; side effects
efectos secundarios
to sign firmar
silence silencio
silk seda
simple sencillo
since desde
sincere sincero
to sing cantar
singer cantante (m/f)

single (bed) sencillo,
(unmarried) soltero
sink lavabo
sir señor (m)
sirloin solomillo
sister hermana
sister-in-law cuñada
to sit down sentarse
situation situación (f)
size (clothes) talla,
(shoes) número ,
tamaño
to skate patinar
skating patinaje (m)
to ski esquiar
skiing esquí (m); cross
country skiing esquí de
fondo (m)
skin piel (f)
skinny flaco
skirt falda
to sleep dormir
slim delgado
slow lento
small pequeño
smart elegante
to smell oler
smell olor (m)
to smile sonreír
smoking fumar
smooth suave
snail caracol (m)
to sneeze estornudar
to snore roncar
to snow nevar; it's
snowing nieva
so tan
soap opera telenovela
software company
empresa de software
soldier soldado (m/f)
solid robusto
some algún/alguna

something algo
sometimes a veces
son hijo
song canción (f)
son-in-law yerno
soon enseguida
sorry: I'm sorry lo siento
south sur (m)
South América Sudamérica
spacious amplio, espacioso
Spain España
Spanish español(a)
sparkling espumoso
to speak hablar
special especial
speciality especialidad (f)
to spend (money) gastar
to spend (time) pasar
spider araña
spirit espíritu (m)
spirits (drink) bebidas alcohólicas, licores
spokesperson portavoz (m/f)
sport deporte (m)
spouse esposo/a
spreadsheet hoja de cálculo
spring primavera
square plaza, (adj) cuadrado
squid calamar (m)
to start comenzar, empezar
starter entrante (m)
station estación (f)
to stay quedar, quedarse, alojarse
steep empinado
stepdaughter hijastra

stepson hijastro
still aún, todavía
to stir mezclar, revolver
stock caldo
stockbroker agente (m/f) de bolsa
stomach estómago;
stomach ache dolor (m) de estómago
stone piedra
stony pedregoso
storage room trastero
store planta, piso
storm tormenta
straight recto, (hair) liso, heterosexual
straight ahead todo recto
straightaway enseguida, inmediatamente
street calle (f)
stress estrés (m)
strict estricto
striking llamativo
strong fuerte
stubborn terco
studies estudios
to study estudiar
stupid tonto
success éxito; to be successful tener éxito
to suffocate ahogar
to suggest sugerir
suit traje (m)
suitable apto
suitcase maleta
summer verano; to spend the summer veranear
sun sol (m)
to sunbathe tomar el sol
sunburn quemaduras de sol

sunglasses gafas de sol
sunny soleado
sunstroke insolación (f)
superb magnífico
supermarket supermercado
supplement suplemento
to support (team) apoyar
supporter hincha (m/f)
to surf navegar; to surf the net navegar por Internet
surgeon cirujano/a
surname apellido
surprise sorpresa
to surprise sorprender
surrounding area alrededores (m pl)
survey sondeo
to suspect sospechar
sweet dulce
to swim nadar
swimming natación (f)
swimming-pool piscina
to switch off apagar
to switch on encender
system sistema (m)

T
tablet (IT) tableta
tablet (med) pastilla
tactful discreto
tactless indiscreto
to take coger, tomar
to take care of cuidar
to take out sacar
to take place tener lugar
talented hábil
to talk hablar
tall alto
to taste probar

to teach enseñar
teacher profesor(a)
team equipo
technician técnico/a
tedious pesado
teeth dientes
(m pl), (molars) muelas
telecommunications
telecomunicaciones
telephone teléfono;
mobile móvil (m)
to tell decir (pp dicho)
temperature fiebre (f),
temperatura
to tempt tentar
tennis tenis (m)
terrace terraza
terraced adosado
terrible terrible
terror miedo
terrorist terrorista (m/f)
to thank agradecer
that eso/esa/ese; that
one aquel/aquella
theatre teatro
then luego, después,
entonces
there ahí; just over
there ahí mismo
there is, there are hay
these estos/as
they ellos, ellas
thin delgado, flaco
to think pensar
thirsty: to be thirsty
tener sed
this esto/esta; this one
este/esta
those aquellos/as
thoughtful amable
to threaten amenazar
thrilling emocionante
throat garganta
ticket entrada, (for

transport) billete (m)
to tidy up arreglar,
ordenar
to tie (draw) empatar
time tiempo, hora, vez
(f); free time tiempo
libre
time: to have a good
time pasarlo bien
timetable horario
tin can lata
tiny pequeñito,
chiquito
tired cansado; to be
tired tener sueño
toast (drink) brindis (m)
to toast (drink) brindar
today hoy
toe dedo (del pie)
together juntos
toilets aseos, baños
to tolerate tolerar
tomorrow mañana
tongue lengua
too, too much (adv)
demasiado
too much/many (adj)
demasiado
tooth diente (m)
totally totalmente
to touch tocar
tour operator operador
(m) de viajes, operador
(m) turístico
tourism turismo
tourist turista (m/f),
turístico/a (adj)
tour guide guía (m/f)
turístico/a
touristy turístico
town ciudad (f)
town hall
ayuntamiento
traditional tradicional

traffic lights semáforo
tragic trágico
train tren (m)
trainer entrenador(a)
training formación (f)
trash basura; empty the
trash tirar la basura
to travel viajar
travel agency agencia
de viajes
travel agent agente
(m/f) de viajes
trekking senderismo
trip viaje (m)
to trip tropezar
trousers pantalones (m
pl), pantalón (m)
true verdadero
trustworthy fiable
truth verdad (f)
to try on probarse
to turn girar
to turn off apagar
TV tele(visión) (f)
twins gemelos
type tipo
typical típico

U
ugly feo
uncle tío
to understand
comprender, entender
to undo deshacer
to undress desvestirse
unemployed
desempleado, parado,
en paro
unfortunate
desafortunado
unique único
United States Estados
Unidos (m pl)
university universidad
(f)

unless a menos que
to unload descargar
unpleasant antipático,
desagradable
unspoilt puro
until hasta
unusual raro
to update actualizar
to upload subir
upstairs arriba
urban urbano
USA Estados Unidos
(m pl)
to use usar, utilizar
useful útil
user name nombre (m)
de usuario
usually normalmente

V
to vacuum aspirar
valley valle (m)
various diversos
VAT IVA (m)
vegan vegano
vegetables verdura
vegetarian vegetariano
to verify verificar,
comprobar
very muy
very well fenomenal
view vista
villa chalet (m)
village pueblo
vintage gran reserva
to visit visitar
visit visita
visitor visitante (m/f)
vitamin vitamina
volcanic volcánico
volcano volcán (m)
to vomit vomitar
to vote votar
voter votante (m/f)

W
to wait esperar
to wake up despertar,
despertarse
to walk andar, caminar,
pasear, dar un paseo,
pasearse
walking senderismo
wallet cartera
to want querer
warehouse almacén
(m)
to wash lavar
washing machine
lavadora
water skiing esquí
acuático
waterproof
impermeable
we nosotros/nosotras
weather clima (m)
web designer
diseñador(a) de
páginas web
webpage página web
website sitio web
wedding boda
week semana
weekend fin (m) de
semana
to weigh pesar
weight peso
weightlifting halterofilia
weights pesas
welcome bienvenido
welcoming acogedor
well bien
well (then) pues,
bueno, entonces
well known famoso
well-equipped bien
equipado
well-kept bien cuidado
west oeste (m)

whale ballena
what? ¿qué? ¿cuál?
wheat trigo
wheel rueda
when cuando
when? ¿cuándo?
where donde, adonde
where? ¿dónde?
which que; which?
¿cuál?
which one(s)? ¿cuál(es)?
while, whilst mientras
to whistle silbar, chiflar
white blanco
who quien, que
who? ¿quién(es)?
why? ¿por qué?
wide ancho
wife mujer (f)
to win ganar
wind viento
wine vino; wine tasting
cata de vinos
wine: red wine vino
tinto
winery bodega
winter invierno
to wipe limpiar
to wish for desear
with con
with me conmigo
with you contigo
to withdraw sacar
woman mujer (f)
to wonder preguntarse
wonderful maravilloso
wooded boscoso
wool lana
word palabra; in other
words o sea
to work trabajar
to work (function)
funcionar
working day jornada

world mundo
to worry preocuparse
worse peor
worst el/la peor
to write escribir (pp
escrito)

Y
to yawn bostezar
year año

yellow amarillo
yes sí
yesterday ayer
yet todavía, ya
you tú, usted, vosotros/
vosotras, ustedes
young joven
your tu/tus, su/sus,
vuestro/a/os/as
youth juventud (f)

Z
zip cremallera